Stepping
Stones

A LIFE OF ART AND ADVENTURE

Stepping Stones

FLAVIA ORMOND

UNICORN

For
Emily and Jocelyn

Contents

Acknowledgements

I would particularly like to thank Emily Ormond Cozens and Jocelyn Ormond for their encouragement and editing of my memoir, and to thank their families for their patience.

I would like to thank the following friends and relations too for their help in myriad ways: Lyulph Avebury, Laura Blom, David Boyle, Richard Boyle, Spencer Cozens, Frank Dabell, Charlotte Gere, Alex Grant, Brian and Sarah Grant Duff, Sarah Goldschmied, Celia Hayley, Elizabeth Llewellyn, Andrew Newman, Penelope Newsome, Richard Ormond, Elizabeth Oustinoff, Jemima Pitman, Ursula Rimbotti, Victoria Schofield and Ursula Walker.

I am most grateful to the National Gallery for allowing me to include photographs of Beaumont study trips.

I would also like to thank the team at Unicorn Publishing Group, in particular Lord Strathcarron, and the designer Vivian Head.

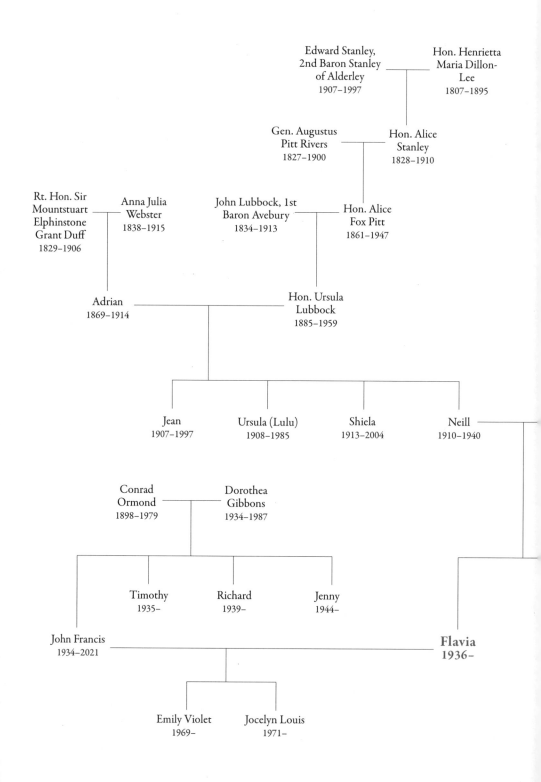

Family Tree

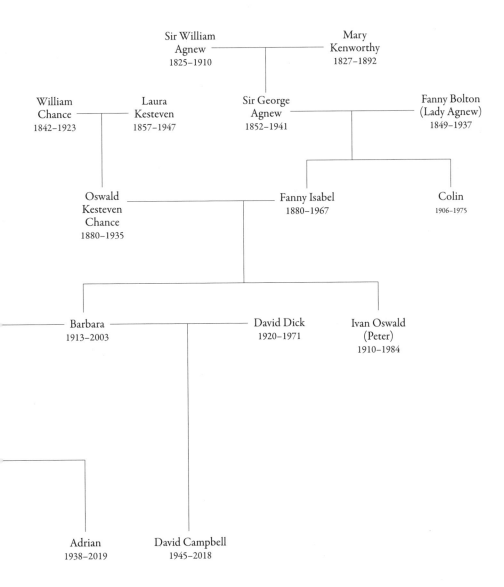

Sir William Agnew 1825–1910 — Mary Kenworthy 1827–1892

William Chance 1842–1923 — Laura Kesteven 1857–1947

Sir George Agnew 1852–1941 — Fanny Bolton (Lady Agnew) 1849–1937

Oswald Kesteven Chance 1880–1935 — Fanny Isabel 1880–1967

Colin 1906–1975

Barbara 1913–2003 — David Dick 1920–1971

Ivan Oswald (Peter) 1910–1984

Adrian 1938–2019

David Campbell 1945–2018

Introduction

Why should I write this memoir? First for myself, for I feel I have run with life like someone with a kite: I have been too keen on excitement and adventure to ever take stock and reflect on the merits of what I have done. My children have also asked me to write it because of the variety of my experiences. I never wanted to stay in a single furrow but to aim higher and further, moving from one experience to another like crossing a brook on stepping stones. Furthermore, the expectations of my generation and background have been so profoundly influenced by the historical events of the twentieth century, and the social upheaval that came out of them, that it seemed important to record my own responses.

I was determined not to have a conventional married life, and in that I have succeeded. My husband John and I have travelled an unusual path together, exploring life and the world through a shared passion for art which led us on remarkable journeys.

Taken to Canada at the age of four as an evacuee in the Second World War, having (although I did not know it at the time) already lost my father, I have never really felt at home anywhere. From an early age, I did not like living in Canada, where our life was unstimulating and repetitive. The Canadians who helped and supported us had given us a very warm welcome, but I had not expected to remain there after the war ended. I longed to be part of the 'Old World' I had been born into. My growing-up years were spent in isolation from my roots, and my mother rarely talked about the past. Life in a small Canadian town was worlds away from the lives of our forebears and family in England.

Now, I feel I am a foreigner wherever I go. I am often taken for an Italian, because of my name and Celtic looks, but more often for an American or Canadian because of my accent. I am never thought to be British. People are confused by my objective attitude towards the country I consider my own. Not having spent my childhood here, I shall always be an outsider.

CHAPTER 1

The Agnews of Bond Street

Thomas Agnew & Sons, a highly successful firm of art dealers in London after 1860, was founded in Manchester by my mother's family. They traded in Old Masters and contemporary paintings, as well as important prints. Art was a recurrent subject of conversation in my mother's household, particularly in relation to Italy, where they frequently travelled. My mother, unusually for her time, studied at The Courtauld Institute of Art during its first year in 1932, before she met and married my father. She and her brother, Peter Chance, together with my grandmother, were formative influences on my own lifelong passion for art.

Thomas Agnew & Sons began trading in Manchester through an antiques dealer called Vittore Zanetti, best known for his work carving and gilding frames. He also presented an annual exhibition of Old Master paintings, probably imported from Italy. In 1817, Zanetti took on as a partner the young Thomas Agnew (of Scottish descent, whose father had moved his family to Liverpool). Thomas gave the firm a new focus by concentrating on their print-publishing activities. Eventually, he took over full control of the company and became one of Britain's leading print sellers. He was also, briefly, the Mayor of Salford. His sons William and Thomas later joined the firm.

William, my great-great-grandfather, had even more flair and turned the Manchester firm into a thriving business selling Old Master pictures. He opened a second branch in Liverpool in 1859 and, the following year, established himself in London at 5 Waterloo Place. Fifteen years later, he moved again, to the site of an old coaching yard, and opened a large gallery at what is today 4 Old Bond Street, where the gallery remained until 2013. William's shrewdness and energy easily dominated the auction rooms and the art market. Working with a number of discerning collectors, he sold pictures to such notable figures as Edward Cecil Guinness, 1st Earl of Iveagh, whose collection hangs on the walls of Kenwood House on Hampstead Heath.[1]

A Lancashire Member of Parliament and one of the founders of the National Liberal Club, William was naturally gregarious. He was a friend of two prime ministers, Mr. Gladstone and Lord Rosebery, on the one hand, and many contemporary artists on the other, including Lord Leighton, Millais and Burne-Jones. He entertained lavishly, both at his country house, Sumner Hill, near Salford and at Great Stanhope Street in London's West End. His sons, George and Morland, were in awe of him. He may not have been as great a connoisseur as his son Morland and grandson Colin would be but he had a natural instinct for anticipating taste. In the year of his retirement (1895), William received a baronetcy from Lord Rosebery, primarily for his enormous contribution to the art world.[2]

When William retired in December 1895, he was quite lost without the excitement of the firm. However, he took his granddaughter Bel (Fanny Isabel, my grandmother) to Rome that winter. Apparently, the family saw this trip as a solution to the problem of their being 'in trade'; this stigma had prevented my grandmother from being presented at Court. Bel, no doubt, had a much better time travelling with her grandfather, and she used to reminisce about this trip. They returned with a fine copy of the Giovanni Bellini *Madonna and Child* in the Galleria Borghese collection. William had been much impressed by the young copyist's skill and had bought it on the spot. My grandmother always had it hanging in her house and, after her death, my mother had it sent to Canada.[3]

William's eldest son, George (my great-grandfather) was chosen to manage the Manchester branch, which he did until his retirement in 1902. George became a great expert in eighteenth-century English mezzotints and created his own fine collection, which was to hang, ceiling to floor, on the walls of his dark green dining room at Rougham Hall in Suffolk. This was the large nineteenth-century house designed in a Gothic Tudor style that he had acquired when he inherited the baronetcy. He also became MP for Salford but preferred the pheasant shooting on his new estate and the company of his children and their families. Pride in 'the firm' united the brothers and sisters and all were expected to contribute to its survival. My mother used to say that the family reminded her of Galsworthy's *Forsyte Saga*. My grandmother and her sisters always took me to Agnew's current exhibition whenever I was in England. It was almost a ritual, followed by lunch at the Hunt Club – one of many smart ladies' clubs still going in the 1960s.

George had eight children, including two sets of female twins. Anthony, his eldest son, had a mental disability, so his second son, Jack, was chosen to run the Rougham estate and his third, Colin, to join the firm after coming down from Cambridge in 1906. Colin was to work with his father's younger brother, Morland, who was considered a great connoisseur of pictures.[5]

Golden wedding anniversary of Sir George and Lady Agnew
at Rougham Hall, 1928 (see Footnote 4 for key)

Colin, my grandmother's younger brother, was passionate from childhood about works of art and had haunted the National Gallery and the Fitzwilliam Museum. His grandfather, William, had also encouraged him by taking him all over Europe. In late 1907, as the only member of the firm who spoke German, Colin was asked to organise a loan exhibition in Berlin of English pictures from English private collections. This exhibition was to include Gainsborough's *Blue Boy* (now in the Huntington Art Museum, Los Angeles). The idea of this show was encouraged by King Edward VII and Kaiser Wilhelm II to alleviate the growing diplomatic tension between their countries. In Berlin, Colin became a close friend of Dr. Wilhelm von Bode, Director of the Kaiser Friedrich Museum (since renamed the Bode Museum). Bode suggested that Colin open a branch of Agnew's in Berlin, in the fashionable Unter den Linden; he had already bought many pictures in England and saw a branch of 'the firm' on his doorstep as a great advantage. Colin made other interesting friends in Berlin, including Max Friedländer, a curator at the Kaiser Friedrich Museum and important for his intensive study of early Netherlandish painting. He also met the distinguished drawings collectors Frits Lugt and his wife Jacoba (who later founded the Institut Néerlandais in Paris).

During these years before 1914, Colin made two long visits to Russia and opened negotiations with the distinguished Yusupov family in St Petersburg. Sadly, he failed to secure the purchase of their two remarkable Rembrandt portraits. However, he was very fortunate to see this magnificent collection before the Revolution.[6]

The Berlin office was forced to close with the advent of the First World War. However, Colin, invalided out of the British army in 1916, went off to New York and worked through some of the dealers there. In 1925, the firm opened a branch on 57th Street, and for the next five years, Colin was to spend every winter and spring there, selling to private collectors and major museums.[7] He also created a market in Canada through The National Gallery in Ottawa and private collectors in Montreal. The Great Depression and the Second World War brought this phase of the business to an end. During the Blitz, Colin and his cousin Gerald kept the London gallery open by day and fire-watched by night.

Uncle Colin was very fond of his sister Bel (my grandmother), and also of my mother Barbara. He came to stay with us in Canada after the war, when visiting various clients. My brother Adrian and I were given explicit instructions on how we were to behave in the presence of such a sophisticated great-uncle. He was tiny, like our grandmother, immaculately dressed and very kind. Years later, I remember dining at his flat in Flood Street with my husband John. Candlelight made his collection of small gold-ground pictures glow on the walls. His flat underlined Bode's influence on Colin's taste – the concept of pictures, furniture, bronzes, ceramics in juxtaposition – a *Gesamtkunstwerk*. In 1951, when our mother first brought us back to England after the war, Colin invited us all to the theatre to see *A Winter's Tale* with Sir John Gielgud. I had never been moved to tears by a play before. Afterwards, we dined at the glamorous Savoy Grill, where the dance floor suddenly rose up in front of us. At fifteen and twelve, respectively, Adrian and I were totally dazzled. This was still the era of ration books, but Colin always sent orders back if they were not up to his expectations. He also liked thick cream poured over ice cream, which I found very strange.

For his holidays, Colin went to the continent, and most especially to Italy. His constant travelling companion was Horace Buttery, who nobly carried the luggage and dealt with practical problems en route. September was always spent at the Lido in Venice. An elegant, sensitive and fastidious connoisseur, Colin had many friends, including the eminent art historians Bernard Berenson and

Kenneth Clark. The latter gave the Address at Colin's memorial service in St James's Piccadilly on 25 November 1975.

My mother's mother, Bel, was the eldest of Sir George Agnew's first set of twin daughters. She was sent as a boarder to St Andrews School in Scotland where she survived the cold by playing hockey and becoming head girl. She told me that, as a young adult, she rode with the Hunt and loved parties. However, when she finally chose a husband, the family was disappointed. She met Oswald Kesteven Chance at a ball in the Assembly Rooms at Bury St Edmunds, somewhat reminiscent of a Jane Austen novel, when he was Adjutant of the Suffolk Yeomanry between September 1906 and May 1907. Oswald was not considered a good match for Bel when they married in 1909, although he was an officer in the 5th (Royal Irish) Lancers, and had fought in the Boer War (notably at the relief of Ladysmith). He later rose to the rank of Brigadier General but the family was dismayed because he had no real interest in the arts.

My uncle Peter was born in 1910 and my mother in Dublin in 1913, during their father's posting there. After the First World War, their father's army career was dealt a fatal blow when my grandmother refused to accompany him to India.

Barbara and Peter, with their grandfather Sir George Agnew,
in the garden at Rougham

She could not bear to leave her very young children behind, and he was thus forced to resign his commission. He tried business in the City, but this was not a success. My mother and Uncle Peter barely spoke of him, and if they did, they called him 'The General'. My mother said he always teased her and made her feel inadequate. He died the year before I was born.

The Chance family ran a successful glass manufacturing firm in the Midlands. Uncle Peter hated to talk about it, although he and my mother were intrigued by the Chances' descent from the De Peysters, one of the oldest families in New York. He and my mother much preferred their Agnew roots, and they spent much of their childhood at the Agnew family seat at Rougham Hall, which they adored; the atmosphere exuded a love of works of art.

1: Amongst other famous collectors, he looked after Alfred de Beit in New York, John G. Johnson in Washington, Alfred de Rothschild, Henry Clay Frick, and George Salting, who left an important bequest to The National Gallery in London.

2: See p. 39, *Agnew's 1817–1967*, Geoffrey Agnew; The Bradbury Agnew Press Limited, 44 Saffron Hill, London EC1.

3: After my mother's death in 2003, it was, sadly, sold.

4: Agnew golden wedding anniversary key:

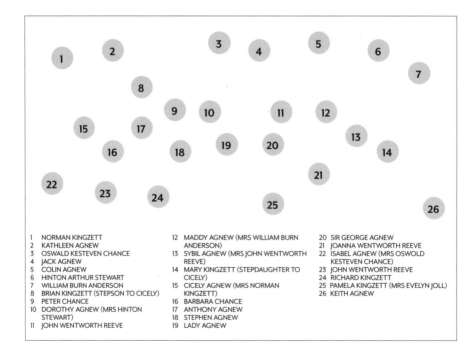

1 NORMAN KINGZETT	12 MADDY AGNEW (MRS WILLIAM BURN ANDERSON)	20 SIR GEORGE AGNEW
2 KATHLEEN AGNEW	13 SYBIL AGNEW (MRS JOHN WENTWORTH REEVE)	21 JOANNA WENTWORTH REEVE
3 OSWALD KESTEVEN CHANCE	14 MARY KINGZETT (STEPDAUGHTER TO CICELY)	22 ISABEL AGNEW (MRS OSWOLD KESTEVEN CHANCE)
4 JACK AGNEW	15 CICELY AGNEW (MRS NORMAN KINGZETT)	23 JOHN WENTWORTH REEVE
5 COLIN AGNEW	16 BARBARA CHANCE	24 RICHARD KINGZETT
6 HINTON ARTHUR STEWART	17 ANTHONY AGNEW	25 PAMELA KINGZETT (MRS EVELYN JOLL)
7 WILLIAM BURN ANDERSON	18 STEPHEN AGNEW	26 KEITH AGNEW
8 BRIAN KINGZETT (STEPSON TO CICELY)	19 LADY AGNEW	
9 PETER CHANCE		
10 DOROTHY AGNEW (MRS HINTON STEWART)		
11 JOHN WENTWORTH REEVE		

5: Morland was the grandfather of the Agnew's director, Geoffrey Agnew, and great-grandfather of the subsequent director, Julian Agnew.

6: After the Russian Revolution of 1917, the portraits were sold to the American collector Joseph E. Widener, by Felix, the last Yusupov, who had succeeded in getting them to Paris. Ref. p. 98 and p. 102, *Great Private Collections of Imperial Russia*, Oleg Yakovlevich Neverov; Vendome Press (Thames and Hudson), 2004. These companion portraits, *Portrait of a Lady with an Ostrich-Feather Fan*, and *Portrait of a Gentleman with a Tall Hat and Gloves*, are now in the National Gallery of Art, Washington DC.

7 : Despite intense competition from the famous art dealer Joseph Duveen, whom he secretly admired, he sold pictures to Julius Bache, J. Pierrepont Morgan, the Newberrys and the Whitcombs, all eminent collectors.

CHAPTER 2

The Pitt Rivers and the Aveburys

On my father's side, I must begin my story with my great-great-grandfather, Lieutenant-General Augustus Henry Lane Fox, later Lane Fox Pitt Rivers (1827–1900). Augustus began life as a soldier but moved on to become a central figure in the development of modern British archaeology.

Augustus entered the army at eighteen because that was what was expected of a younger son, but his military career was undistinguished and his rank on retiring merely honorary. However, an interest in both archaeology and ethnology had begun during his army postings overseas, and he slowly amassed a considerable collection of ancient objects from various parts of the world, collecting primarily everyday artefacts and assembling them meticulously into sequences to illustrate ideas of evolution.

Aged only twenty-two, Augustus married Alice Stanley, the eldest daughter of Sir Edward Stanley, 2nd Baron Stanley of Alderley and Henrietta Maria, daughter of the 13th Viscount Dillon. Stanley was a distinguished politician and cabinet minister who served under successive prime ministers and notably established the Post Office Savings Bank. Henrietta was seriously interested in girls' education at a time when it was generally considered of little importance, and she became one of the founders of the Girls' Public Day School Trust and of Girton College, Cambridge, where she established the library that bears the Stanley name. She also made sure that the college was not allowed a chapel during her lifetime – so that the remaining funds could pay for more professors and more books.

Augustus was not considered a great match for Alice, whose family was very grand, if eccentric. Poor Alice was her mother's least favourite child and, sadly, this was made obvious. Her sisters married rather better than she: Blanche, later the great-grandmother of the Mitford sisters, to the 5th Earl of Airlie; Kate, the mother of the philosopher Bertrand Russell, to Viscount Amberley; and Rosalind, to the 9th Earl of Carlisle, who owned Castle Howard, John Vanbrugh's baroque masterpiece in North Yorkshire.

Augustus and Alice were initially very short of money and largely dependent on the income from his army commission. However, in 1880 Augustus unexpectedly inherited the Rivers estate on the death of his cousin, Horace Pitt Rivers, 6th Baron Rivers, on condition that he took the surname Pitt Rivers and the arms of the Pitt family within one year of taking possession. In London, they were able to move from Earl's Court to the smarter address of 4 Grosvenor Gardens and, in the country, to the remote seat of Rushmore on the extensive Cranborne Chase estate in Dorset. Through this stroke of good fortune, Augustus progressed from being a relatively penniless soldier to being able to follow his interests and achieve an elevated position in the scientific world of his time.

Cranborne Chase was known to have important earthworks dating back to the Neolithic Age. Augustus, now Lane Fox Pitt Rivers, gave up 'society' and spent every spare penny of his inheritance on digging. At Cranborne Chase, he managed to examine over forty sites (including Wor Barrow, South Lodge Camp and Woodcutts). To explore the links between archaeology and anthropology, Augustus had rejected the fashionable obsession with burial mounds and their treasures in favour of hillforts and settlement sites. He viewed archaeology as an extension of anthropology – a groundbreaking approach at the time.[1]

In 1884, Augustus gave the University of Oxford his large collection of ethnographic objects; by the end of his life, he had collected over 50,000 of them. He insisted on a purpose-built museum with a specialised curator, also a groundbreaking concept in its time. This was the Pitt Rivers Museum. His son-in-law and colleague Sir John Lubbock described the collection that made up this new museum as 'perhaps one of the finest collections in the world', and another of his colleagues, Edward Burnett Tylor, called it 'one of the best contributions made by Englishmen to the study of culture'. Methods of understanding past human civilisations have, of course, been under major review in recent decades, and the Pitt Rivers Museum is nowadays at the centre of that discussion. This would probably have delighted Pitt Rivers, who wrote the following to Tylor in 1883: 'I look upon my museum as being in no way an exception from the ordinary laws affecting all human affairs in regard to development, and that so far from considering it perfect as it is, I cannot conceive any idea of finality in a Museum of the kind.'[2]

Alice, with whom Augustus had nine children, was not noted for her interest in her husband's scientific career. In her book *The Stanleys of Alderley*[3], Nancy Mitford described Alice's family as 'rude, quarrelsome and lively'. This description certainly fitted my great-grandmother, who was Alice's third daughter and sixth child. Also called Alice, she was known as 'Granlin' by all her great-grandchildren. She married her father's colleague, Sir John Lubbock, who was later created Lord Avebury and, like her father, was a prominent archaeologist as well as a natural historian. It was said that she accepted the hand of this much older man to escape from home and her father, the often irascible Augustus.

Alice Fox Pitt and John Lubbock met at a house party at Castle Howard. (Her eccentric aunt, Lady Carlisle, was reputed to have emptied the entire contents of her husband's wine cellar into the castle's moat. She believed in temperance!) The youthful Alice had come down late to breakfast and had been fiercely scolded before the rest of the party rose from their chairs and left the room – all except the kind widower, Sir John Lubbock, who stayed to keep her company and 'attend to her wants'.[4]

John Lubbock was a neighbour of Charles Darwin in Kent and, although Darwin was a generation older, they became close friends. The Lubbock family owned a large country house called High Elms, near Farnborough. The Darwins lived in a more modest house in Downe, the nearest village. Their properties abutted, and the two men would meet daily, the young Lubbock walking through the 'home woods' to Darwin's house. After the outcry caused by Darwin's *On the Origin of Species*, published in 1859, Lubbock became one of his greatest supporters. He felt obliged to move his patronage from the church at Downe to the church at Farnborough, as Darwin was no longer welcome at Downe due to his scientific revelations.

The Lubbocks were bankers. At the age of fourteen, John Lubbock went into the City firm of Robarts, Lubbock & Co, a bank that was eventually absorbed into what is now Coutts & Co.[5] He had been at Eton, but he was a delicate child, and, in any case, Eton did not cater for his scientific interests in botany, entomology and astronomy. (The last was heavily encouraged by his father, Sir John William Lubbock, a successful partner in the family bank whose real interests lay in being an astronomer and mathematician. He had studied the eighteen-year cycle of the moon and its effect on the tides, and a group of craters on the moon is named after him.)[6]

Lubbock's diaries show that he missed companions of his own age but, more significantly, they demonstrate his discipline and self-determination in organising his time for study, work and social entertainment. A famous family story relates that he even wore elastic-sided boots to avoid the time wasted on doing up laces. He never wasted a minute and read avidly on the train to the City each morning. He was quoted as saying, 'a man must always have a book in his pocket'. My mother frequently drew our attention to this quotation in her constant encouragement to her children to read more.

Reading through the list of Lubbock's achievements in adult life, one is acutely aware of his enormous energy. It seems remarkable that he ever had time to spend with his family. Like his father-in-law Pitt Rivers, he was invited to join all the distinguished scientific societies – so many that his family observed that he could be at an annual general meeting every day. Darwin had introduced him to a number of eminent thinkers, and he became one of the nine members of the elite X Club, a dining club devoted to science 'untrammelled by religious dogmas'.[7] The members firmly upheld the theory of natural selection in the face of theological opposition.

In 1856, at the age of twenty-two, Lubbock was made a partner at the bank. At around that time, he met Ellen Hordern and, when they married two years later, he brought her to live at High Elms. Marriage did not interrupt Lubbock's busy life! He became the Liberal MP for Maidstone in 1870 and later became famous for introducing the Bank Holiday, then popularly referred to as 'Saint Lubbock's Day'. As a keen archaeologist, he invented the terms 'Paleolithic' and 'Neolithic'. He was also deeply concerned with the protection of ancient monuments, introducing in 1881 the Parliamentary Bill which saved so many of them. He bought the village of Avebury to prevent the villagers from constructing cottages in stone pilfered from its ancient stone circle. He also acquired Silbury Hill, the extraordinary archaeological mound nearby, built between about 2400 and 2300 BC.[8] Lubbock inherited the baronetcy on his father's death in 1865 and in 1900 was made a hereditary peer. He chose Avebury for his title. Ellen's son John, the eldest of their five children, was to become the second Lord Avebury.

Lubbock, always concerned about the 'working man', was determined to reduce his labour and improve his educational benefits. On this front, he was well supported by Ellen and Mrs. Darwin. The latter insisted on keeping the school room open at Downe for local workers to use as a reading room on winter nights. Lubbock eventually became Principal of the Working Men's College, a position he held from 1893 to 1898.

On my eleventh birthday, my grandmother, Ursula (Lubbock's daughter), sent two of his books to me in faraway Canada, titled *The Uses of Life* and *The Pleasures of Life*. These philosophical anthologies, still in print today, were widely read for Lubbock's thoughts on life gathered from his extensive reading on many different subjects. My grandmother hoped they would form the basis of my personal library. At the time, I was not sure my standard of knowledge would ever be up to this challenge, but I have always kept her inscribed copies on my bookshelf. I was actually more fascinated by Lubbock's intense scientific study of the daily life of ants, bees and wasps – another interest fostered by the influence of Charles Darwin. He discovered that bees preferred the colour blue, and he had a famous pet wasp which lived for twelve years and was given an obituary in *The Times* when it died.

Punch's *Fancy Portraits* (No. 97) published the following verse about Lubbock in 1882, which neatly encapsulates many of his activities:

> *How does the Banking Busy Bee*
> *Improve his shining Hours?*
> *By studying on Bank Holidays*
> *Strange insects and Wild Flowers!*

In 1883, Lubbock decided to move on from insects to domestic animals and acquired a black terrier puppy called Van which he planned to teach to read. Cards were inscribed with the words 'food', 'tea,' 'bone' and 'water'. After ten days, success seemed to have been achieved and Van could apparently select the correct card for a particular item. Prime Minister William Gladstone, when invited to High Elms for the weekend, showed great interest in the dog's progress and Lubbock published reports of Van's achievement in the *Spectator* and *Nature*.

When Lubbock first met my great-grandmother, Alice Fox Pitt, at Castle Howard, he found her to be good company: she was highly intelligent, witty and amusing. Since his first wife Ellen's death in 1879, he had been lonely. He married Alice, who was twenty-nine years younger, in 1884. For a project on their honeymoon in France and Switzerland, they collected and recorded wildflowers. It seems that Lubbock could never just be idle! Despite being so much older than Alice, Lubbock is supposed to have been very youthful and was noted for 'the beautiful serenity of his mind'.[9]

Unfortunately, Constance and Gertrude, adult daughters from Lubbock's first marriage, still lived at High Elms. Alice was similar in age to them and was always bitterly jealous of them. They, in turn, referred to her as their father's 'ancient monument'. Lubbock apparently did little to address this situation except to immerse himself in his multiple interests.

My grandmother, Ursula Lubbock, in fancy dress

Alice's first child Ursula (my grandmother) was born in 1885, six weeks early owing to one of the many terrible quarrels between Alice and her stepdaughters. Luckily, Ursula would always be very close to her father, and they would go off on excursions together even when she was only a child of eight. Lubbock's great friend Sir Mountstuart Grant Duff, later to be Ursula's father-in-law, records their botany expeditions in his diaries. He would bring along his own daughter, Lily, who was about the same age as Ursula. When Ursula was old enough, she became her father's secretary. She also shared his interest in, and support of, the Liberal Party.[10]

Lubbock had always suffered from a weak chest, and to protect it, he grew a beard. In later life, his chest became a serious problem and Alice decided they must find a house on the North Sea. They bought and extensively renovated Kingsgate Castle, perched on the chalk cliffs near Broadstairs on the Isle of Thanet. It had wonderful views, a secret passage to the beach (with steps which are said to have inspired the title of John Buchan's famous novel, *The Thirty-Nine Steps*) and bedroom doors each painted with the name of one of Lubbock's scientific friends, including Grant Duff. They moved into the castle in 1903, and Lubbock died there in 1913. Alice and her stepson, John, who became the 2nd Lord Avebury, kept the castle until 1922. They also shared High Elms until John's death in 1929. John had never married, and only two or three years separated them in age. Alice, ever imperious, had refused to relinquish her title and settle for 'the Dowager Lady Avebury'. Society found their relationship very puzzling.

While still at Kingsgate, John sold off some of the land to their neighbour, press baron Lord Northcliffe, owner of the *Daily Mail* and *Daily Mirror*, who wanted to extend his golf course. Alice was furious, and when they finally decided to sell the castle itself, she refused to let Northcliffe have it. It went to a hotel group instead. Adrian and I were taken to see Kingsgate by my father's eldest sister, Jean, in 1951. The names of Lubbock's scientific friends were still on the bedroom doors, and I remember gazing reverently at 'GRANT DUFF'.

After John's death, Alice tried to share High Elms with the 3rd Lord Avebury. Also John, he was the son of her eldest son Harold, and her eldest grandson. He was considered very wild. He not only married three times but also tried to make a large part of the property into a track for car racing. Alice was again so angry that she tried to disinherit him, insofar as she could, by giving High Elms and all the land to Kent County Council. She then took out a lease on the house and gardens for her lifetime, and lived on there until her death in 1947. Apparently, John's charm was immense; according to my father's second sister, Lulu, all three of his former wives turned up at his funeral in June 1971.

1: Pitt Rivers was elected to The Royal Society and also became a member of the Ethnological Society, the Society of Antiquaries and the Anthropological Society. Both Pitt Rivers and John Lubbock, his future son-in-law, knew Charles Darwin well and all three were part of a group of 19th-century British archaeologists determined to establish the early history of the human race.

2: Letter to Tylor, 5 February 1883, L106 Salisbury and South Wiltshire Museum Pitt Rivers Papers, ref. Pitt Rivers Museum website.

3: *The Stanleys of Alderley, Their Letters between the Years 1851–1865* (1939), edited by Nancy Mitford.

4: *Life of Sir John Lubbock*, Horace G. Hutchinson, (1914) London: Macmillan and Co; Vol.1, p. 207.

5: Robarts, Lubbock & Co was established in 1772. The bank had created the Lubbock family fortune, through the industrial revolution and the building of Empire.

6: The main crater, in *Mare Fecunditatis*, is 'Lubbock A' and some of the principal satellite craters – about eleven – are also listed under his name. He won the Royal Society Medal for his work on tides in 1833. He was also a Visitor to Greenwich, a title which appears to have conferred some say on how the Observatory was run.

7: Thomas Archer Hirst, private journal, 6 November 1864. Hirst, one of the club's founding members, described its first meeting: 'On Thursday evening Nov. 3rd, an event, probably of some importance, occurred at the St George's Hotel, Albemarle Street. A new club was formed of eight members: viz: Tyndall, Hooker, Huxley, Busk, Frankland, Spencer, Lubbock and myself. Besides personal friendship, the bond that united us was devotion to Science, pure and free, untrammelled by religious dogmas.'

 8: The creation of this hill, of chalk and clay, built in stages between 2400 and 2300 BC, had involved incredible technical skill. It is still owned by the Lubbock family. Both Avebury and Silbury Hill are UNESCO sites.

9: Hutchinson, op. cit.

10: It is poignant, in view of the family's tragic losses in the First World War, that in November 1905, Lord Avebury, together with Lord Courtney of Penwith, founded an Anglo-German Friendship Committee which sought to counteract the influence of anti-German propaganda in Britain, then at its height.

CHAPTER 3

The Grant Duffs in India

James Cunningham Grant Duff, another of my paternal great-great-grandfathers and the father of Lubbock's good friend Mountstuart, was destined for a career in India. He was born James Grant in 1789 at Eden, a large house on an extensive estate near Banff in Aberdeenshire. Duff and Cunningham were names added at a later date to make it possible for James, like Augustus Pitt Rivers, to inherit more landed estates.

Educated in Aberdeen, James accepted a cadetship at the age of sixteen and sailed for Bombay. He joined the Bombay Grenadiers and took part in the storming of Maliah in 1808. His abilities attracted the attention of the twenty-four-year old Mountstuart Elphinstone, British Resident at Poona. Elphinstone lived an ascetic life and was a solitary figure who could be found reading Sophocles or the Persian poets as early as four in the morning. James became his assistant and friend and eventually named his eldest son after him. Elphinstone believed that 'education was the remedy for all the ills of Indian society',[1] and he could see that James understood intuitively how best to communicate with the local people. Elphinstone's idea was that Indians should be trained as good civil servants but that the British should maintain military and political power. This was deemed an acceptable idea at that time. James was promoted to captain and Elphinstone appointed him British Resident at Satara, a centre of the warlike Mahratta tribes. From family papers we understand that James was expected to negotiate with the Mahratta Peshwa, Baji Rao II, who had captured the Raja of Satara in 1818. Under James's skilful leadership, with only one European colleague and a body of Indian infantry for support, the Rajah was rescued and eventually allowed to take back direct rule of his territory.

Despite his success in India, James decided to return to Scotland when he was only thirty-three. The Indian climate and the stressful life had affected his health. On arrival at Eden, he married the daughter of Sir Whitelaw Ainslie, who had been British Resident in Madras. The Ainslies owned Delgatie Castle, not far from Eden (dating back to the sixteenth century and now open to the public). My mother and father stayed at Delgatie in the early days of their marriage. My mother told me the bath was in the old dungeon and the whole place was very 'creepy' at night, especially as they only had candles for light.

James's final triumph came with writing *A History of the Mahrattas* in three large volumes. Not only had he collected much material through his access to state papers but he also drew on local family and temple archives and his personal acquaintance with the Mahratta chiefs. The history was translated into the major languages of western India, becoming required reading for Indian students during the British Raj, and is still read by students of Indian history.[2]

James was devoted to his mother-in-law and his daughters but never cared much for his wife or his two sons. His eldest son followed in his footsteps in India while the second son, Ainslie, eventually inherited Delgatie. James quietly cultivated his estates for the remainder of his life, and died in 1858.[3]

James's eldest son, Mountstuart Elphinstone Grant Duff (named after James's benefactor), was my great-grandfather. His was a lonely childhood, and he spent his time exploring the countryside around Eden. As a result, he became a passionate botanist. He went to school in Edinburgh and then to Balliol College, Oxford. From the age of eighteen, he kept a diary and wrote in it every day of his life. In the published version (1851–1901) he states that, 'I carefully eliminated from it almost all reference to the working part of my life'. Thus, regrettably, one learns little about the man except that he was gregarious and belonged to a number of dining clubs. At Oxford, he was influenced by the Oxford Movement and developed a lasting friendship with the future Cardinal Newman. He took a second class degree and was called to the bar – but his interest lay in politics.

The diaries recount how he enjoyed meeting his many friends at breakfast parties. Among these friends was my great-grandfather John Lubbock, a fellow botanist. Mountstuart was also a member of the Liberal party and held the parliamentary seat for Elgin Burghs until 1881. He met Anna Julia Webster at a party, and married her after only six meetings. Their wedding was immediately followed by a return to Eden so he could fight and win another election. He was noted for his conscientious efforts to enlighten his constituents with lectures on foreign politics, travelling to the continent to clarify his ideas. It was not surprising that his two eldest sons, Arthur and Evelyn, should become diplomats.[4]

In 1877, the Grant Duffs moved to York House on the Thames at Twickenham, where Mountstuart could invite distinguished friends to parties. Both Gladstone and Disraeli were frequent visitors to this house. As a Member

No. 48   STATESMEN, No. 33.   Price 6d.
" A philosophic liberal."

Mountstuart Elphinstone Grant Duff MP – *Vanity Fair*, 1869

of Parliament, Mountstuart was considered 'too philosophical and too subtle to suit the taste of the ordinary British legislator'.[5] His career was not helped by weak eyesight (he was usually read to) and a thin, high-pitched voice. Under Gladstone's prime ministership, he was, however, given the post of Under-Secretary of State for India and, later, for the Colonies.

My brother and I were brought up on the story of his successful appointment as Governor of Madras (1881 to 1886). Even our mother was impressed by this appointment. As Governor, he was particularly noted for his creation of the Broadwalk along the seafront, modelled after a Sicilian 'Marina'. Otherwise, his time there was, in fact, somewhat difficult: administration, it appears, was never his strong point.

Nevertheless, his great interest in botany thrived. He hired a local draughtsman to draw all the indigenous plants in the area. This project took two years, undertaken at Mountstuart's own expense.[6]

Anna Julia and some of their children accompanied Mountstuart to India. Tiny, the eldest daughter, described her father as red-bearded with very bright blue eyes. He was apparently bored by all children and said, 'Vanish, vanish!' whenever he saw one of his own. Adrian, my grandfather, was the third of his four sons. The two eldest sons, Arthur and Evelyn, were both diplomats. Adrian was to join the army and the fourth son, Hampden, became a sailor.

Hampden never married but lived on his own in a small flat in South Kensington. I can remember meeting him on our first return to England from Canada in 1951. I was fascinated by his warm, sparkling eyes and the tattoos on his arms which he showed to me and my brother Adrian with great pride. Our very conventional Canadian childhood had not prepared us for the eccentricities of the Grant Duffs. We also met our grandfather's sisters, Lily and Iseult (a psychoanalyst of some distinction) that summer; lunch was arranged at Lily's house in Aldeburgh. I remember thinking they were so old and so strange, and I was surprised by their interest in us. Lily had reddish hair, cropped like a man's, and Iseult, her father's intense blue eyes. Both wore very old-fashioned summer dresses with large floral patterns. Granny Chance, my mother's mother (about whom I say more in the next chapter), who accompanied us, was a remarkable contrast in her elegant, if slightly shabby, 'pre-war' tweed suit.

Tiny, the eldest daughter, was ten when Mountstuart was given his post in India. She described their departure from London as a great occasion. Her parents bought lovely new clothes for her and her favourite sister, Dot, and gave a big farewell afternoon dance which they were allowed to attend. When the Grant Duffs set sail for Bombay, they were seen off at Tilbury by their grandmother and the three elder sons, who were to stay at school in England. Lily, the baby, was also left behind with cousins but Hampden was fortunate enough to be included, with his nurse. The fifth daughter, Iseult, was born in India and was very much a child of the Raj. Many years later, she returned to India as a Christian missionary but decided there was a conflict between

Christianity and the British Empire. She decided to give up Christianity!

Mountstuart was socially in his element as Governor of Madras. He gave his first levee, at Government House, four days after his arrival, and Anna Julia her first reception. Many parties followed. After one year, Mountstuart recorded that he had hosted 1,089 guests to dinner, had travelled 4,875 miles and had got to know 250 new plants.[7]

My husband John and I went to Madras many years later to follow in Mountstuart's footsteps. Our Indian guide was deeply impressed that I was a direct descendant of his and went to great trouble to get us permission to visit Government House. It had been taken over by the Naval Ministry and piles of dusty papers filled most of the state rooms. The despondent clerks sat cross-legged on the floor at traditional low desks. Quite a different atmosphere, we imagined, from the pomp of Mountstuart's era.

Upon his return to England, Mountstuart gave up his active political life for one of literary and scientific pursuits with friends such as John Lubbock. He became President of the Royal Geographical Society and the Royal Historical Society, was elected to the Royal Society and appointed a trustee of the British Museum. He died in London in 1906.

1: When Elphinstone later served as the Governor of Bombay from 1819 to 1827, he was instrumental in setting up educational institutions for the local population, which led to the foundation of state education in India.

2: The three Mahratta Wars were fought between the British East India Company and the Mahratta Empire between 1775 and 1818. The British were victorious and thus gained control of most of India.

3: James's uniform was eventually given to the National Army Museum, Chelsea, by Aunt Lulu, his great-granddaughter. Today, sadly, due to the reorganisation of the museum, it can only be viewed by prior request.

4: Arthur, the eldest, was successively Minister to Cuba, Peru and Ecuador, Chile, and Sweden and was awarded the Grand Cross of the Order of the Star of the North by the Swedish Government. Evelyn was Secretary of Legation in Tehran during the Persian Constitutional Revolution and allowed 12,000 Iranians to take sanctuary in the Legation gardens, to the fury of the Foreign Secretary Sir Edward Grey.

5: cf. *Times* obituary, 1906.

6: Sadly, these portfolios/albums eventually disappeared into the London sale rooms.

7: Whilst Mountstuart and Anna Julia were in Madras, the children were taken to Guindy, the country residence not far from the city. The gardens were beautiful, and there were exotic flowers growing everywhere. In the stables there were a hundred horses. 'The stables were kept like a drawing room and the horses polished with the naked hand.' (Anne Fremantle, *Three-Cornered Heart*, The Viking Press, 1971, p. 39.)

CHAPTER 4

My Grandfather, Adrian

My Grant Duff grandfather, Adrian, was born in 1869. At the age of fourteen, he was sent to Wellington College and then on to Sandhurst. As the third son, it was assumed he would become a soldier, with a duty to defend King and Country, the glory of his regiment and the British Empire. His ambition was to be a fearless officer in the famously courageous Scottish fighting force, the Black Watch. I can remember his half-length portrait in uniform, executed in oils, hanging in the drawing-room at my grandmother Ursula's house in Mulberry Walk, Chelsea. It seemed to demand the same veneration as a precious Greek icon. Adrian is shown as a handsome Lieutenant Colonel in his late forties, highly intelligent and accomplished. It was painted by his friend Walter Sickert from a hand-painted photograph, made into a miniature.[1] Both works must have been presented to my grandmother in commemoration of Adrian's death in France at the outset of the First World War.

Initially, there was no vacancy in the 1st Battalion Black Watch so Adrian was sent to Belfast to join the 2nd Battalion. In March 1890, he happily transferred to the 1st and was immediately sent to Gibraltar. His extensive diaries show that he was gregarious, like his father, Mountstuart, and famous in his regiment for teaching reels and playing the piano and bagpipes. However, he was also easily bored and longed for active service. After a brief stay in Egypt and Mauritius, he arrived in Cape Colony in August 1894 for an 18-month tour of duty.[2]

While in South Africa, Adrian fell madly in love with Agnes van de Byl, whom he met through an old Wellington friend. The Van de Byls were an old Cape Dutch family who owned 'Morningstar', a large wine-growing estate just outside Cape Town. The beautiful Dutch-style house, surrounded by a

Miniature of Adrian Grant Duff, 1914

large garden and vineyards, is still there, although under completely different ownership. John and I spent a morning there on our South African tour in September 2012, retracing the footsteps of my grandfather.

Unfortunately, Adrian's hopes of love and marriage were thwarted. Agnes was still at school and considered too young for a formal engagement. When Adrian moved on to India, they were still writing to each other, much to the displeasure of Agnes's schoolmistress. However, in 1899, Adrian was devastated by a letter from her sister with the news that Agnes was to become Mrs Parminter instead. She married a British officer of the 8th Foot, so their paths crossed again in England after Adrian had married my grandmother. Adrian was thrilled when he was asked to be godfather to their son.[3]

He wrote bitterly in his diaries about this South African love affair. His marriage to Granny, aged only twenty-one, would not be for another ten years, when he was forty.

Before going to India, Adrian returned to England for a short period. Already, he feared his military career was stagnating, and he decided to take a course in tactics. Upon rejoining the 1st Battalion in Subathu,[4] he deemed this posting so tedious that he gave up writing his diary for the next three years. Luckily for him, this period did cover active service. Following the loss of the Khyber Pass in late August 1897, and the subsequent revolt of the local tribes of the North-West Frontier, Adrian was appointed Commandant of the Base Depot for the Tirah Expeditionary Force based in Peshawar (now in modern-day Pakistan but then part of British India). For his exemplary service, Adrian was decorated with the Tirah Medal with clasp and promoted to captain. Nevertheless, in 1900 his Indian 'day' merely consisted of parade before or often after breakfast, polo three days a week, and sometimes games of hockey. One can understand the frustration of a soldier who longed for action. Queen Victoria died while Adrian was still in India and he is recorded as saying, 'she leaves a world in tears'.

Finally, on 13 November 1900, having offered itself for active service in South Africa, the 1st Black Watch received orders to join the Boer War, then at its height. Adrian was thrilled to move into action at last and took part in campaigns in the Transvaal and Orange River Colony. He subsequently received the Queen's South Africa Medal with two clasps.

Adrian's regiment returned to England in September 1902, following which he enrolled in the Staff College. Appointed Staff Captain and General Staff Officer, he was promoted to Major in 1907. Never idle, he also qualified as an interpreter in French. During this period, he married my grandmother Ursula Lubbock, with whom he had four children including my father. Army life was a very big adjustment for Ursula after the Edwardian comfort of High Elms. At least her father, John Lubbock, and father-in-law Mountstuart Grant Duff, were great friends and Adrian a supportive husband and companion.

I find it very unsettling that Adrian seemed to have such an appetite for action which, ultimately, meant war. However, there was a deepening readiness for war across Europe in the early 1900s, particularly among the educated elite. It was not about 'bloodthirsty calls for violence against another state, but rather of a "defensive patriotism" that encompassed the possibility of war without necessarily welcoming it.'[5]

Adrian was part of this elite, and he was highly acclaimed for his extensive work on *The War Book*, which set out the way in which Great Britain would mobilise in the event of war. From 1910 to 1913 he was seconded to the War Office, and in 1913 he was awarded the C.B. (Companion of the Most Honourable Order of the Bath) in recognition of his designing and editing of *The War Book*.[6]

In August 1913, Adrian eagerly rejoined his regiment as Lieutenant Colonel, and in May 1914 he took command of the 1st Battalion of the Black Watch, stationed at Oudenarde Barracks in Aldershot. He was a natural leader, and at last his goal had been achieved.[7]

On 14 September, he was killed while leading his men against the German army at the Battle of the Aisne. On the morning of the battle, the British Expeditionary Force had not realised that a very large German force, with heavy artillery, was entrenched on the ridge above the Chemin des Dames.[8] During the night, there had been heavy rain followed by thick mist. By eleven o'clock that morning, the first assault upon the Chemin des Dames had failed and the battalions were shattered. Battalion commanders, including Adrian, immediately began to reorganise the remnants of their units in a desperate effort to lead them forward in another assault. Under continuous shelling, Adrian reorganised the ranks and distributed ammunition himself. It has been noted that he was much appreciated by the men for his concern for their welfare. During the ensuing attack, Adrian was fatally wounded in the stomach. His adjutant, Lieutenant Guy Rowan-Hamilton, was nearby and supervised his rescue down a steep hill to a cave. He was placed on a bed of straw and a doctor was called. Adrian insisted that Rowan-Hamilton go back to the firing line but when he returned later, Adrian was dead.[9]

The War Office sent a formal letter to my grandmother, dated 5 February 1915, which informed her that Adrian was buried in the centre of the cemetery at Moulins – a large wooden cross marking his grave. Today, that cross has been replaced in stone.[10] In 1940, Adrian's son Neill was also buried in a cemetery in northern France. My grandmother, Ursula, spent the rest of her life returning to these graves.

1: On the back of the miniature's case, there is the name and address of a well-known contemporary photographer: 'Walter Jones, 196 Sloane Street SW'.

2: It is interesting to note here that his grandfather, James Cunningham Grant Duff (of Mahratta fame) had been a part of the force which wrenched Cape Town from the Dutch. The British needed this strategic port to refuel their ships.

3: The two families kept in touch through Aunt Jean, Adrian's eldest daughter. The son, Charles Parminter, settled in New Zealand in later life, and when our cousin, Ursula Walker (née Boyle), went to live there in 1961, her social standing was assured through this smart connection.

4: Subathu was a hill cantonment in Simla District, Punjab – now Himachal Pradesh. It was created by the British Army in the mid-19th century for families and troops to escape the heat of the plains.

5: *The Sleepwalkers: How Europe Went to War in 1914*, Christopher Clark; Penguin Books, 2013, p. 237.

6: As Assistant Military Secretary to the Committee of Imperial Defence, Adrian was responsible for the complete instructions to each Government Department for its procedure on the outbreak of war. In the second edition, he extended the system to all parts of the Empire.

7: Despite Adrian's enormous dedication, the Government gave the credit for *The War Book* to Sir Maurice Hankey, who, as head of the Secretariat of the Committee of Imperial Defence, was responsible for its application when war broke out. My grandmother was justifiably very upset and wrote in *The Bond of Sacrifice* (Vol. 1, 1914): 'it was Colonel Grant Duff who constructed the detailed plan and, with the help of many others, did most of the work which saved this country from chaos in August 1914 – through the smoothness and success with which his arrangements worked out.'

At the end of his life, Maurice Hankey paid public tribute to Adrian Grant Duff, his colleague at the Committee of Imperial Defence.

8: Chemin des Dames is an old Roman road named in honour of Louis XV's daughters (whose carriages would pass that way), which overlooks the Aisne valley.

9: Richard Boyle, *Adrian Grant Duff*; Real Press, 2014; and Victoria Schofield, *The Black Watch: Fighting in the Front Line 1899–2006*; Head of Zeus, 2017, p. 47.

10: Adrian is deeply remembered today by the Black Watch Association as one of the great commanders in France at the First Battle of the Aisne and was commemorated in 2014 on the centenary of the battle at the memorial site of Black Watch Corner in Flanders.

CHAPTER 5

My Grandmother, Ursula

With secret misgivings but much encouragement from her parents, Ursula Lubbock married Adrian Grant Duff in October 1906. He was about twenty years older than she. She had been working happily at home as her father's secretary, so this decision completely transformed her life.

Writing to her youngest daughter, Shiela, in August 1937, Ursula admitted that 'I was terrified of life until I met Daddy – he gave me confidence in everything and the feeling that no outside thing could really hurt one at all.' She and Adrian spent their honeymoon in Italy. Ursula told her children how she had removed her hot dress and worn her mackintosh over her petticoat, to sightsee in comfort.

Ursula was a spirited young woman used to the intellectual circle of her father's friends – and especially the scientists, who made a special effort to converse with the children, as she noted in her essay 'Yet another Victorian Childhood'. Consequently, when Adrian returned to the regiment in August 1909 after the births of my aunts Jean (1907) and Lulu (1908), and was posted to Limerick, Ursula was miserable. She wrote to her mother of 'exile in Limerick' and how her loneliness and boredom were only occasionally alleviated by 'The Black Watch performing exquisite music such as *Kiss me over the hedge, honey.*'

Fortunately, they returned to London a year later, and my father Neill was born the following October. Both parents adored their children and took them out on educational expeditions to places like the London Zoological Gardens. Shiela was born in early May 1913, and the following September, they all went to the Oudenarde Barracks at Aldershot, where Ursula was even more heavily committed to the duties of an Army officer's wife. She wrote to her mother in October 1913, 'I have to start formally at once about the women and it seems soon I shall be saddled with Committees and associations and even the thought of it is rather bewildering...', and, in December: 'I am struggling with the Regimental Christmas Tree things and getting so bored with it.' In March 1914, she wrote again to her mother, 'Sunday is the only quiet day I have with Adrian. He is so busy other days he just comes in for meals.' And on 23 March, she wrote to say, 'Things do look very bad though as far as the army is concerned Adrian says a great deal of mischief has already been done which can probably never be undone.... Winston [Churchill] seems to have done rather more harm than usual.'[1]

Adrian took command of the regiment in May 1914, and from another letter in June, we gather he was working so hard that Ursula only saw him at intervals when he dashed in to change his clothes. In August, she wrote that she 'see[s] no alternative to war due to the behaviour of the Germans'. In early September, when the war broke out, she immediately sent the children to High Elms. Adrian was killed only two weeks later; it took another week for the tragic news to reach her.

Poor Ursula joined her children at High Elms, and Nunn, her former lady's maid, took up the role of Nanny. My father was not yet four and his younger sister, Shiela, only one. Ursula recorded how upset Neill was by his father's death and how he continued to miss him by talking about the son he would eventually have himself.

They moved into one of the newly built neo-Tudor houses in Mulberry Walk, Chelsea, bought for Ursula by the trustees of Adrian's estate. Such houses were not considered grand in those days. Chelsea was not a fashionable area: there were slums amid the artists' studios on the south side of the Kings Road. Granlin, Ursula's mother, still owned the large family house at 31 Cadogan Square, off Sloane Street – a much smarter address, from which Aunts Jean and Lulu were eventually married.

The children loved High Elms, and school holidays were largely spent there with hordes of other cousins and their parents. The grand house parties were now a thing of the past. Shiela recorded[2] how they were all allowed to visit their grandmother (Granlin), and then Uncle Johnny (the second Lord Avebury), whilst they were having their breakfasts in bed. They also loved to stay with Granlin at Kingsgate Castle on the Kent coast.

Ursula, brought up in an aristocratic Edwardian household, had been so bored by the interminable meals in her parents' dining-room that she used to knit under the table. When her mother made her wear low-cut dresses at evening parties, she would stuff a linen table napkin down her bosom to minimise the bareness. Once she showed me how their escorts at balls used to rub up the girls' cheeks to make a bewitching flush. Cosmetics were out of the question. It must have been at this time that she wrote *A Mere Woman's Notebook*, a cynical account of the vapid thoughts of her female contemporaries which was eventually published privately. Ursula was not only unconventional by nature but also a remarkably modern woman who should have gone up to Oxford like all the Lubbock men. She must have felt so fulfilled when three of her children did go there. Jean and Shiela attended Lady Margaret Hall and distinguished themselves in French and Philosophy, Politics and Economics, respectively. My father, at Balliol, was much less academically minded but deeply interested in politics and philosophy.

Ursula was a prolific reader and letter writer who made the most of London's five posts a day. She seldom used the expensive telephone. Later, she used to complain to my mother that my brother Adrian and I did not date our letters, making it difficult to keep up an accurate correspondence with us. Had she lived in the twenty-first century, her passion for keeping in touch with people and exchanging ideas would have been greatly enhanced by the use of emails and social media.

As advocates for what they thought would be a more perfect world, Ursula and Adrian became members of the Eugenics Society in 1907. Adrian initially introduced her to the eugenics cause, believing that it was essential to create a strong breed of people in the educated class who would make good 'officer material' for the future of the army. He lived in a world of privilege in which it was assumed that young men from the 'working class' would seldom have the chance to rise through the ranks. While they were stationed at Aldershot in May 1914, Ursula had received a letter from Major Leonard Darwin, one of Charles Darwin's younger sons, asking her to write to her MP about the importance of eugenics. Although she considered replying to it, she pointed out to her mother that, not having the vote, she could not really claim to have an MP. Her sharp sense of humour always rose to the occasion.

On becoming a widow, Ursula worked under the influence of Carlos Blacker, a psychiatrist and long-term birth control advocate who became General Secretary of the Eugenics Society. As a doctor, he had seen those people worst affected by frequent childbearing and overlarge families. At that bleak moment, just after the First World War, many poor families lived in Chelsea a short distance from Mulberry Walk. Ursula was intensely affected by their miserable lives and wrote a biting short story, *The White Rats*, which aimed to illustrate that eugenics and birth control could alleviate their poverty. In it, a mother – probably Ursula – tells her two small daughters (probably my aunts Jean and Lulu) that rather than have pet rats, they should adopt a local family to love and look after: '...somehow it did not seem quite like peace or quite right that the children should have white rats. And so she suggested ... that perhaps it might be better, and just as much fun, if each child adopted a family of real children and tried to give them some happiness and pleasure.' However, one child adopts a 'Eugenic' family and the other a 'Dysgenic' family which is dysfunctional, with too many children in poor health and a refusal to consider birth control. In the end, she says that there is no hope for the Dysgenic family, whereas, 'The Eugenic family ... so soon became self-reliant that they afforded no scope or interest to the child who had adopted them'. This unpublished story, which has survived in family papers, had good intentions but now seems naïve and cruel.[3]

Ursula and Cora Brooking Sanders Hodson (a well-known American writer on eugenics, and secretary of the London Eugenics Society) came to be described as 'politically moderate, humanitarian-minded figures who saw eugenics as a way to improve the world in the difficult interwar period'.[4] In 1934, Granny, always an idealist, visited a 'racial hygiene' exhibition in Berlin, when it was becoming evident that the idea of 'racial hygiene' was completely perverted. By 1938, however, Granny had become so anti-Nazi that Carlos Blacker had to beg her to refrain from protesting in one of his meetings. In September 1939, she received a letter from Dr. Maurice Newfield in which he wrote, 'there is a world of difference between the eugenics taught by Galton [Sir Francis Galton, follower of Charles Darwin] and the doctrine labelled with the same name in Nazi Germany'.[5] Anyone with misgivings about Ursula's views on eugenics should also take into account that at this date she turned her attention to helping Jewish refugees whose families were being exterminated by the Nazis.

What the forward thinkers of Ursula's generation saw as constructive compassion for the human race now looks prejudiced and inhumane. Ursula's approach had some of its roots in the Darwinian theory of natural selection, so much a part of her early life through her father's scientific work and close relationship with Charles Darwin. She died in 1959, when this well-intentioned world was still based on Victorian values of enlightenment. Her Stanley first cousin, the philosopher Bertrand Russell, had actually proposed 'procreation tickets' to protect the gene pool of the elite. Social idealists like George Bernard Shaw supported the idea of selective breeding, and the leading economist John Maynard Keynes was the Society's governing director from 1937 to 1944.

Ursula played an active role in the Eugenics Society in England for the rest of her life. She always kept in touch with the many interesting friends she had made through it including Julian Huxley, Secretary of the Zoological Society. In 1931, the Eugenics Society's letterhead shows Major Leonard Darwin as Honorary President and The Honourable Mrs Grant Duff as one of the two Secretaries.

One is constantly reminded of Lord Avebury's influence on his daughter's life. Her interest in his work was such that in 1924, long after his death, she edited a book of his essays. His involvement with the natural sciences must also have encouraged Ursula to support 'Men of the Trees', the society founded in Africa in 1922 by Richard St Barbe Baker, who had witnessed firsthand the disastrous effects of deforestation in Kenya. The society opened a branch in Britain in 1924 and became a worldwide society in 1932, committed to reforestation around the world. Both Ursula and Sir Shane Leslie, the Irish MP whose son (Sir Jack Leslie) John and I met in Rome years later, were on the London Council and corresponded regularly well into the 1950s. When St Barbe Baker himself became an officer at the London branch, Ursula generously lent him her dining room at Mulberry Walk to use as his London headquarters. Adrian and I were introduced to him in 1951 amid a sea of papers in the dining room. It was a very suitable opportunity for Adrian, who later studied forestry at the University of New Brunswick before working in the logging industry in British Columbia and becoming involved in reforestation in Northwest Canada.

Ursula also took a keen interest in the Liberal Party, thus following in the family tradition. She wrote articles for the *Liberal Bull* and gave public lectures for the Liberal Party cause.

Ursula, known to us as Granny Grant Duff, habitually gave drinks parties at Mulberry Walk, where she would introduce friends and family to each other over glasses of sticky South African sherry. I remember during one such party, held after I had returned to England in the summer of 1954, she heated the hors d'oeuvres in the oven on beautiful Copeland china plates, unconcerned by the burning of the glaze. It was the quality of conversation which mattered to her – not material possessions!

Granny Grant Duff had seventy-two first cousins, including Bertrand

Lord and Lady Avebury with their sons (left to right) Eric, Maurice and Harold Lubbock

Granny Grant Duff at High Elms in her characteristic black hat, with my mother, Barbara, and my father, Neill

Russell and the writer Percy Lubbock. Percy was stepfather to the writer Iris Origo and lived for years at Lerici, near La Spezia in Italy. He went blind towards the end of his life and a series of young men were employed to read to him. My husband John was among them, several years before we met, one of the amazing coincidences of our lives. All these cousins formed the foundation of Granny Grant Duff's extensive social life, although she strongly disapproved of Bertrand Russell's pacifism during the First World War.

Two of Granny Grant Duff's brothers had died in action during the First World War: Eric Lubbock at Ypres in 1917, in the Royal Air Force, and Harold Lubbock at Arras in 1918. Eric was their mother's favourite child, and Granlin never got over his death.

Granny Grant Duff's husband Adrian was killed in 1914, and her only son in 1940. My mother explained that all this tragedy was the reason for Granny's always wearing black. When we returned to England for the first time after the war, in the summer of 1951, my mother recognised Granny's black straw hat as the one she had worn to my parents' wedding in 1934.

Neither Granny Grant Duff nor her mother ever came out of mourning. Their writing paper was always edged in black.

My brother Adrian and I were singled out for special attention that summer. I could see that Adrian made Granny feel closer to our father, Neill. She arranged for us to meet Bernard Fergusson of the Black Watch, who had known our father and had included him in his history of the regiment, *The Black Watch and the King's Enemies*. We were overawed and tongue-tied, as we had never met people, other than immediate family, who had known our father or even knew who he was.

1: At this time, Winston Churchill was the First Lord of the Admiralty and considered too left-wing by Adrian, although they were both Liberals.

2: *The Parting of Ways*, Shiela Grant Duff, Peter Owen Ltd, 1982, p. 20.

3: Letter to Ursula from J Kent Parsons, 7 June 1945, mentioning this story and saying it is unlikely to be publishable.

4: *A Life of Sir Francis Galton. From African Exploration to the Birth of Eugenics*, Nicholas Wright Gillham, Oxford University Press, 2001, pp. 357–358.

5: Sir Francis Galton (1822–1911), who first coined the term 'eugenics' and campaigned vigorously on its behalf, began by extrapolating Darwin's theory of evolution through natural selection to mankind. Galton would have been horrified had he known that, little more than twenty years after his death, forcible sterilisation and murder would be carried out in the name of eugenics.

CHAPTER 6

My Father, Neill

Special love was attached to my father, as he replaced for Granny Grant Duff a husband and two brothers. He was brought up in the atmosphere of the Black Watch. The death of his 'Daddy' was an ever-present sadness for him as a child. At the age of eight, he went to Wagner's School in Chelsea where he was teased for always wearing a Black Watch kilt.

He was not deterred. He went on to Wellington College, following in his father's footsteps, and then to Balliol College, Oxford, (1928–1931) following the family tradition. He was very popular but not inclined to academia; he enjoyed good conversation and playing golf. After leaving Balliol, he spent six months in training as a reservist with the Black Watch before accompanying a 'Public Schools Empire Tour' to South Africa and Southern Rhodesia.

In Southern Rhodesia, he wrote to his sister Shiela, describing his trip to Victoria Falls where he had stayed in the grand colonial hotel. John and I stayed in the same hotel seventy years later – little had changed. However, my father had walked to the falls in the early morning, unimpeded by modern Zimbabwe's security fences. He described the deafening roar of the water, the baboons cavorting about in the lush undergrowth, and the excitement he knew Livingstone would have experienced less than a century earlier. We, instead, were forced into a commercial taxi.

On his way home from South Africa in July 1932, my father joined Shiela, his favourite sister, and her Welsh friend Goronwy Rees – later to become a controversial left-wing journalist – who were on holiday in Germany. It was the moment of the rise of Hitler and they witnessed violence in the streets. They quickly left and joined some Oxford friends in Vienna, and then travelled on to the Soviet Union at the suggestion of Muriel Gardiner, an American acquaintance who had been studying psychoanalysis with Freud in Berlin and had offered to pay for them all to accompany her – by this time, my father, Shiela and Goronwy were virtually penniless.[1]

Shiela was reading Philosophy, Politics and Economics at Oxford, where

Neill in his kilt

one of her deepest friendships was with Goronwy, who was very much in love with her. I met him many years later when we were both staying with Shiela. He kindly spent an entire evening telling me about my 'wonderful father'. I was very touched, as I was always searching for an impression of my father.

In a letter from Shiela to her mother in 1932, she wishes 'Neill had had more friends like Douglas Jay and Goronwy Rees rather than his nice but conventional ones'. She added that my father was always very 'philosophical' in his views on life. That same year, he had become a member of the recently-formed Chatham House, the Royal Institute of International Affairs think tank. Today, it describes itself as providing 'thought leadership on key issues that defined the 20th century'.

Shiela had come to know Douglas Jay just before going up to Oxford. He was a brilliant scholar, a Fellow of All Souls, and he subsequently became an influential Labour MP and Labour Minister. On our trip to England in 1951, Shiela persuaded him to give me and Adrian a cream tea on the terrace of the House of Commons. As usual, we could not think of anything interesting to say, and I felt Aunt Shiela's disappointment. We represented 'the last of the Grant Duffs', as the aunts were always telling us, which only increased our self-consciousness. However, the grandeur of the occasion – and the strawberries and cream – were not lost on us.

Legend has it that my father first met my mother at a dance where they were both taking refuge behind the long curtains. Their deep fondness for each other developed further at a Eugenics Society Ball before which Granny Grant Duff held a dinner party at Mulberry Walk. When my other grandmother asked to which ball my mother was going, there was considerable shock over the response.

My mother once told me how frightened she had been at the Mulberry Walk dinner parties in the Thirties because all the guests argued about politics and she had no idea what to say. My father was very interested in international politics but my mother felt completely out of her depth with the pitch of the arguments. She observed that my father's sister, Shiela, and their mother, both bright and intense and very idealistic, had most unusual and intellectual friends. These included Indians whom they had met in London through Jawaharlal Nehru, then President of the Indian National Congress. Sheila had looked after Nehru, as both secretary and official companion, when he came to London in 1936, three days after the death of King George V. This unforeseen source of friendship led to Shiela's meeting Iqbal Singh, a Punjabi Sikh from Delhi who was a Congress Party member and a journalist and broadcaster. He became a particularly good friend of Shiela's. My husband John and I were to meet him years later at the Congress Club in Delhi. Another, Cedric Dover, was a Eurasian (Anglo-Indian) biologist from Calcutta deeply concerned with the problems of ethnic minorities. Cedric had met my grandmother through the Eugenics Society and would one day write her obituary in the *Eugenics* journal. Adrian and I met both these friends at Mulberry Walk when we came to England in 1951. We were fascinated that Shiela and my grandmother had Indian friends. In those days, Canada was the most unworldly place to grow up in and it was, in any case, unusual in England, in those circles, to have Indian friends. We had heard of Mahatma Gandhi because our mother had told us about the Indian gentleman who drank only orange juice as a protest against his country's being ruled by the British. However, to us he was a very remote figure living in another sphere.

Bronisław (Bronio) Malinowski, now considered to have founded the field of social anthropology, was frequently at dinner. He was the first to seriously study the sex lives of the tribes in New Guinea. He shared many of the interests of Avebury and Darwin, although he met Granny Grant Duff through the Eugenics Society. They maintained an intimate correspondence after he left London to teach at Yale University. Born a citizen of the Austro-Hungarian Empire, he fought on their side in the First World War and moved to America on the eve of the Second World War. My mother said that Bronio had a keen eye for attractive women and was always very kind to her at these dinners. His youngest daughter, Helena, became Granny Grant Duff's ward upon Bronio's death in 1942 and, many years later, a great friend of mine.

My mother came from a relatively conventional family of successful art dealers, and my father from a fairly eccentric intellectual family pursuing forward-looking ideas in the sciences and education and politics. There were concerns in the Grant Duff family about their relationship; Shiela and her mother thought that the Agnews were conventional socialites and that my mother's brother, Peter Chance, who was then employed on the 'front counter' at Christie's, was merely a London dandy. However, Uncle Peter was ambitious at Christie's, and he and my mother had visited Florence and Siena together to absorb and further their knowledge of art and architecture. My mother had actually been one of the first students at the newly founded Courtauld Institute of Art in 1932 although, alas, as was the custom, she gave up her studies after her marriage. Convention still dictated that she spend her days with her mother and mother-in-law, or the aunts, or joined the 'ladies who lunch'.

In order to be in a position to marry my mother, so it would appear from their correspondence, my father went to work in the City as a stockbroker. He was bored by the City but, equally, did not want a career as a soldier. Instead, he sometimes talked about living off the land in a remote part of Scotland. He disliked the artificiality of formal London society yet needed the intellectual stimulation of his London friends. My mother begged him to hang on in the City, as the Agnews were only going to be impressed by a formal career for the man she married. They were both very young and my father had no money of his own.

My parents corresponded constantly through 1933 and their letters reveal their youth and happiness and deep love for each other. Their letters often went back and forth to the Black Watch Barracks at Colchester where my father was a reservist. However, between my father's military service with the Black Watch and my mother's constant filial duty to her grandparents at Rougham Hall, they seemed mainly to meet in London on Saturdays. They were formally engaged in October 1933.

Despite family misgivings, my parents were married in April 1934 and spent their honeymoon in Rome. My father could only afford the airfares to Rome by contracting to book tickets to Mussolini's fascist exhibition, *La Mostra della Rivoluzione fascista 1932-34*, which automatically conferred a discount on the fares. They were obliged to walk through the exhibition to have their discounted travel tickets stamped. My mother told me that my father would not stop and look at any of the exhibits!

Their holidays abroad in the late Thirties included a trip to the Balkans. My father was intrigued by their recent transformation from a turbulent part of the Austro-Hungarian Empire to the modern state of Yugoslavia. It was, no doubt, also an affordable holiday choice, as my mother remembered the bed bugs and their car breaking down! Sometimes they travelled with Shiela, who was working as a journalist for the *Observer* in Prague. Sheila wrote to her mother from Prague on 15 March 1937 saying that she was going to meet Neill and Barbara in Carlsbad, a famous spa town in Czechoslovakia. Otherwise, my father – a keen sportsman – went off on his own to ski in Switzerland and, when at home, to play golf.

In London, my parents lived a fairly enlightened social life. I discovered, nearly thirty years later, that my parents had spent weekends at Virginia Water with their friends George and Nellie Wingfield Digby, who were looking after the Ouspenskys at Lyne Place, Surrey. This house was bought in 1935 by the rich supporters of Ouspensky (1878–1947), the esotericist who was a 'guru' for many intellectuals. His lectures in London were attended by such literary figures as Aldous Huxley and T.S. Eliot, along with other writers and journalists. His influence on the London literary scene of the 1920s and 1930s, as well as on the Russian avant-garde, was considerable. Nellie Wingfield Digby described to me how she and my mother had to slip into the Ouspensky bedroom at six in the morning and entice their dogs to go out for exercise without waking their master and mistress. The ethereal George, Nellie's husband, later chief curator of the Textiles Department at the Victoria and Albert Museum, was given the menial task of painting the greenhouse with my father. My mother never mentioned this experience.

Perhaps she was embarrassed but, in any case, she seldom talked about her life with my father; she had put it behind her – buried it.

Born at 36 Jubilee Place, Chelsea, on 31 January 1936, my first memories begin at the age of three, living from day to day with a bad-tempered nanny on the cold top floor of a big house, at 26 Ormonde Gate, Chelsea. I did not know my mother. Every afternoon at about five, I was dressed in my best and taken down to the drawing room to be presented to my parents, seated in front of a glowing fire. I remember my father very well as he was always so warm and attentive and often produced novelties like 'glitter wax' to amuse me – once, he showed me his electric train laid out in a mysterious upstairs room, and one weekend he took me out to fly a kite. My mother was always present, always elegant, always smiling but never spoke.

This was a typical life for an English upper-class child in the late Thirties. I remember the anxiety of my third birthday party – standing at the top of the stairs and seeing below a sea of unknown faces: the children of my parents' friends. However, there were some high spots. We were often taken to stay with my Agnew great-grandfather, Sir George Agnew, at Rougham in Suffolk. My mother always loved taking us there.

Rougham had huge gardens to explore and a stable yard with a donkey and cart. I remember my grandmother pushing me around in a wheelbarrow and my great-grandfather dancing with me in the library.

I also remember rather frightening trips to High Elms where Granlin, my Avebury great-grandmother, surrounded by little dogs, looked me and my mother up and down with apparent disapproval from her wicker bath chair. She always found fault with my clothes, and always looked for something to criticise. If she saw any of the maids in the hall, she would point her walking stick and exclaim: 'What is that?'. I vividly recall dropping her large and precious Wemyss china pig on the marble floor of the loggia. Of course, it shattered, and I was terrified of the consequences. I can remember repeating over and over again to Granny Grant Duff, who witnessed the event, 'It doesn't matter, it doesn't matter,' to which she firmly responded, 'But it does matter.' However, at the beginning of the war we were firmly invited back to High Elms for our safety. I can just remember the barrage balloons floating in the sky near the house. Several bombs were to fall on the property but not on the house.

After my father's death, the war became a permanent backdrop to our lives. I think I felt about my father's death the way he had felt about the loss of his

Portrait of Barbara, 1934

father. I have always been very possessive about the memory of my father and jealous of my brother, Adrian, with whom I was naturally meant to share his loss. However, I could not share it, and years later when we went to see his grave together, I still could not come to terms with this idea. I had to place my own flowers by the grave and mourn separately, on my own. Even today, since my brother's death, I cannot help feeling – irrationally – that our father was mainly mine. Perhaps this is not entirely irrational, as Adrian was only eighteen months old when our father died and, therefore, had no memory of him.

1: Shiela Grant Duff, op. cit., p. 43.

CHAPTER 7

The Second World War

In the world of 'grown-ups', life was becoming increasingly unnerving. My brother Adrian was born on 20 September 1938, ten days before the Munich Crisis and the publication of Aunt Shiela's bestselling book, *Europe and the Czechs,* in which she argued for the rights of Czechoslovakia and criticised the British appeasement policy. Her book was distributed to all Parliamentarians the day Neville Chamberlain returned from Munich. Another world war was less than a year away.

An interesting letter written by my father to Shiela on 3 October 1938 illustrates acute anxiety over the threat of war and the keen political awareness of my father and his family. They were certainly not unique in their fear of both Bolshevism and National Socialism, but many people were simply hoping that 'appeasement' would ease the threat posed by Hitler's Germany.

I have just been glancing through the *Times.* I have read of Duff Cooper's resignation, Harold Nicholson's Manchester speech and finally the leader 'Munich and after'. It is the point of view of this leader and the people who can agree with it, which fills me not with suspicion and anger, but gloomy foreboding.

In my humble opinion National Socialism stands for something fundamentally different from Christianity, nobody would dispute it. Nat. Soc. is both a system of government, and a philosophical system. It is a tyranny in which people cannot live the lives they want. Democracy if it exists, is a system of government which allows freedom of conscience, freedom of political opinion, freedom of speech, freedom of the press, freedom of the people of the same ideas to congregate etc.........Civilization has been the emergence of ideas based on freedom. Everywhere that freedom is threatened by uncivilized men. We surely know quite well that if 'dictator' countries become commercially and militarily more powerful then their pernicious ideas will spread more than they have already done.........

I do not fully agree with what you say in your letter. I don't think that you can say that 'we' or anyone has betrayed the one people in Europe which was really prepared to stand up for Western ideals [Czechoslovakia]... That is the appalling disaster of the present situation, our policy is based on the belief that what we have done is just. That we can do good by co-operating with evil...

I am often told that Chamberlain's policy is activated by a sincere fear of bolshevism. What does this mean? I have always thought that bolshevism or marxism wished to introduce the millennium by force... National Socialism is exactly the same only that Hitler has racial ideas, and is also the inheritor of Pan-Germanism. Fascism also is the same.

Uncle Peter and his wife Aunt Paddy (Pamela Martin Smith) attended the Olympic Games in Berlin in 1936 as part of their honeymoon. It seems shocking today that British (and American) tourists continued to go to Germany throughout the late 1930s, but they were still revelling in the beautiful music, the fine galleries and the lush countryside Germany was renowned for.

When my mother died in Canada in 2003, I flew out there to help my brothers sort through her possessions. I found a dusty wicker basket of letters hidden under her bed. She had always maintained that letters should not be kept, so I was most surprised. They covered a period of her life she had never wished to talk about, starting with my parents' early letters to each other from 1933, through the autumn of 1939 when they desperately tried to keep in close touch, and concluding with letters written back and forth when my father was in France in the last days of his life. Some of the letters underline the futility of the campaign of the British Expeditionary Force (BEF) in northern France. Unfortunately, there are no letters between 19 January and 23 May 1940 from my father to my mother but two from Granny Grant Duff to Bronio Malinowski, sent on 7 March and 18 April, help fill the gap. I have used all these letters to try and tell the tale of my parents' last months together – mainly apart – before my father's death.

In the small hours of 1 September 1939, German divisions rumbled across the Polish frontier. With this invasion and Britain's declaration of war on Germany on 3 September, life changed forever. My father, as part of the Black Watch Reserve Force, went immediately to the depot in Perth. In a letter to my mother he describes his journey as 'tolerable', as he was offered an unclaimed first-class sleeper for the night. He joined the packed train at Peterborough, having come directly from Rougham with six pieces of luggage. He wrote again to my mother on 5 September, complaining of the 'standing around' and doing nothing. He says in his letter, 'It is all very peaceful and the war so remote.' A letter to my father from Granny Grant Duff, of the same date, implies that my mother was thinking of going up to Perth to be with him. Granny also observes in this letter that my father's thoughts and ideals are like his own father's. One can imagine how she felt about her only son going to war, and I think it must sometimes have been very difficult for my mother to share my father with her and to feel a part of their very close relationship.

The post was so frequent in those days that it is often hard to follow these fast-moving events. Letters and postcards would cross. My father was relocated to Dover after a week in Perth and my mother joined him there. It was decided that we children should go to High Elms in Kent on 12 September so our parents could come and see us from Dover.

There seemed to be considerable concern about the availability of nurse maids to help look after us at High Elms with Granny Grant Duff in charge. I was allowed to go and stay with my mother at Sweet Sultan (seemingly a house in Dover my mother shared with another officer's wife and child). My father wrote to a friend on 13 September from Dover that he had 'been firing a Bren gun on the range today'. He added that he would be 'much happier if

My father and I on bicycles at High Elms, September 1939

My parents at the Clock House, High Elms,
September 1939

[he] could feel that the government really believed that Hitlerism was the devil... the men are confused, cynical and depressed.'

In a letter dated 21 September, Granny Grant Duff told my mother that Granlin, Granny's mother, had invited us to stay on as long we wished at High Elms. She said that Granlin liked having Adrian and me there. Granny certainly did, and I remember her being very companionable. On 29 September, Granny wrote again to our parents, saying that her friend Jeanne Watrelot was still in Armentières, and that she would welcome any of Granny's children who went to France. This information must have been written for the benefit of my father who would be going to France very soon, and indeed he did go to see her. Granny had formed a friendship with the Watrelots when visiting the grave of her husband Adrian after his death in the First World War. My father's visit to the Watrelots seems poignant in light of his own fate.

Granny Grant Duff then offered my mother the use of the Clock House on the High Elms estate – normally used by Aunt Shiela but only sporadically – where my father could join her on leave. My mother agreed to move in there. I remember Aunt Shiela being at her desk there and offering me barley sugar sticks out of her pencil jar.

In early October, my father left for France with the 1st Battalion of the Black Watch, destined (my mother always felt) to follow in his father's footsteps. In December, the Battalion was moved up to the River Saar near the Maginot Line, on France's border with Germany. They were there for three weeks, including Christmas Day. Very sadly, I have only one letter between my father and my mother for the rest of that autumn. On 19 November, he answered one from her, referring to 'Attlee's imbecilities'.[1] He also mentions the problem of what to do with Ormonde Gate, their big London house in Chelsea. He suggests storing the furniture and leaving the house empty.

I do not recollect where we spent Christmas, but at some point, we moved to Virginia Water to stay with the Wingfield Digbys, away from the danger zone of central London. I can remember Granny Grant Duff coming to see us there, riding on a bicycle, with one highly prized banana for us to share, and the Wingfield Digbys' son's Czech nurse being forced to leave in case she was a spy. I also remember very clearly my father coming to say goodbye to me there when I was ill in bed one snowy morning in February. He must have been on leave. I never saw him again.

In early March 1940, the 1st Battalion of the Black Watch was reassigned to the 51st Highland Division, commanded by General Victor Fortune, to replace the territorial battalion of the Black Watch. A letter dated 7 March from Granny to Bronio Malinowski (by now teaching at Yale University) relates that my father had just been home on ten days' leave. She also wrote that she had applied for a permit to go to France at Easter. (She added that Eugenics and Penal Reform and Social Services were lifting their heads again after the first shock of war.) In April, my father had a second tour of the Saar with the 51st. Granny wrote again to Bronio, saying that she had gone to France at Easter for eight days – spending one day in Paris and the rest of the time with the Watrelots at Armentières near the Belgian border. She saw my father but not Robert Boyle, her daughter Lulu's husband, who was on the staff of General Gort, commander of the BEF. Uncle Robert 'had been coming home for leave on 12th – but all leave stopped of course'.[2] That Granny was able to see my father seems incredible, as he was on active duty. She had been very fortunate to get her permit in those final days of the so-called 'Phoney War'. The tide was about to turn.

The last letters exchanged between my parents were sent in May 1940, beginning with one on 23 May. My father wrote to my mother to say he was now with another company of the battalion and that the 51st Highland Division had retaken Cambrai. He expressed some confidence that the Germans might be withdrawing at this point, although it was said by some that the German army had enough food for seven years. He described spending two nights in a wood near a nightingale's nest, and how loudly the birds sang. He added that 'the talk in the mess is all about the length of the war, slavery, the freedom of speech and so on'. They were just sitting and waiting, as there was really no news of the actual fighting. It is likely that his letters were also subject to censorship at this point. On 24 May he wrote again, telling my mother of a French cartoon showing two soldiers riding a tandem bicycle. They are stopped by a [French] general who asks the first where he is going: 'to the Front with orders, my general', he replies. When the general turns to the one riding behind, the answer is, 'I have the counter order, my general.' The cartoon refers, of course, to the confusion of that campaign.

In a letter dated 25 May, my father mentioned the idea of emigrating to Vancouver Island after the war, living on the land and raising a large family. He suggested sending out Uncle Hampden 'to buy a property and keep it warm for us' (Hampden was the rather solitary but kindly younger brother of his father Adrian). This letter may have been the reason for my mother telling Adrian and me that our father had wanted to go to Canada after the war. Certainly it was given as a reason for our staying there for good.

On 26 May, my father wrote that he was very busy commanding his company and thus unable to read my mother's last half-dozen letters which he had been carrying around for twelve hours in his pocket. He observed that the situation was very unlike 'what they thought it would be'. His very last letter to my mother, dated 29 May, was, alas, only about asking her to send hair oil for his very dry scalp and more about his uncomfortable army boots and moving camp. By this time (probably unknown to my father and his company) the evacuation of the BEF and other Allied forces from Dunkirk was underway and the Battle of France was almost over. Rather than retiring northwards towards Dunkirk, the 51st Highland Division, including the 1st

Battalion of the Black Watch, was ordered to withdraw westwards to secure the northern end of the retreating French line. It was encircled, outside the small seaside town of Saint-Valery-en-Caux, by the German 7th Panzer Division commanded by General Rommel. The nearly indestructible tanks of this German division had moved astonishingly swiftly through Belgium via the Ardennes Forest, assumed to be an impenetrable barrier by the Allies, and swept across Normandy with the intention of completely cutting off the British army from the French coast.

From a letter written to Granny Grant Duff in December 1940, we know that on 9 June my father saw his old school friend, Captain John Lindsay, who was with the 8th Argyll and Sutherland Highlanders. They knew each other from their London childhood at the Wagner School and in the Wolf Cubs. Lindsay wrote:

I saw him for a few minutes on the 9th June. The Division had had a lot of heavy fighting when I joined the 8th [Argyll] on the 7th on the Bresle. About midnight on the 8th June we withdrew in lorries (when almost surrounded I believe) to the Bethune just East of Dieppe. I was guiding our Battalion when we came to a 'T' road and had to turn right. The Black Watch in front of us should have turned left but turned right instead and were turning their lorries round in the road. This blocked the road for us so I went to look for a Black Watch Officer to see how soon we could get on and ran into Neill. We passed the time of day until the road block was cleared.

Lindsay observed that 'Neill was looking well but dead tired due to very little sleep for days for any of them.' They promised to look each other up again in more peaceful times.

This letter shows the chaos caused by the 'blitzkrieg' ('lightning war') being waged by the German tank divisions. The 8th Argyll was withdrawn that night, and (despite heavy losses) many of its soldiers were lucky enough to reach Dunkirk and be evacuated. Sadly, the Black Watch, which had been in the same brigade, was now in another division with different orders. Shortly after this, on 8/9 June, the Black Watch was completely surrounded by the Germans.

My father was killed three days later, in the early morning of 12 June, just outside the village of Houdetot and eight miles from Saint-Valery-en-Caux, while leading his company (under the command of Colonel Honeyman) against the German tanks. His company had been cut off from the main force of the 51st Highland Division which, under the leadership of General Fortune, was fighting a retreat to the coast at Saint-Valery-en-Caux. His company never received word that General Fortune had agreed to surrender to Rommel.

In my mother's wicker basket, another group of letters forwarded from Granny Grant Duff to my mother, now an evacuee in Canada with my brother and me and our Boyle cousins, tells the tale of her desperate attempts to find out what had happened to her only, beloved son, now reported 'missing'. Granny had written to everyone connected with my father, the 51st Division and the 1st Battalion Black Watch in Normandy that morning of 12 June. Postcards from Granny to my mother in Canada, written on 26 and 27 July, indicate that she had so far been unsuccessful in finding out what had happened. It was hoped that he was a prisoner of war, as the surviving members of his division had all been captured.[3]

During the rest of the summer and autumn of 1940, Granny spent most of her time, between air raids over London, dashing frantically to the letterbox.

The first letter in answer to Granny's enquiries came from General Fortune's wife on 2 August, saying: 'no word about anyone through yet except Major Thomas Rennie, who escaped and is due home on 4th August so he will be able to tell us about those [who survived] in whose camp he was'.

And, indeed, in the wicker basket there is a letter from Major Thomas Rennie to Brigadier General Guy Rowan-Hamilton (son of the friend who had tried to save the life of Adrian Grant Duff twenty-six years earlier), dated 13 August and written after his amazing escape to England. It was sent on to Granny Grant Duff, who forwarded it to my mother in Canada after making a careful copy. (Granny made written copies of everything for fear of loss in the post.) Rennie had been taken prisoner at Saint-Valery-en-Caux and had escaped from the group, with a fellow officer, in a wood when they were being marched from Bethune to Lille. They finally got home by train through Spain and Portugal and a flight home from Lisbon. They escaped on 21 June and did not reach London until 4 August. Rennie begins the letter with '*it was all rather a tragic affair losing all those officers and men. They were first class material and the Division did magnificently to the end. But for our wretched allies, we would have been clear but I suppose the Entente had to be kept up to the end.*' The letter does not refer to what happened to my father.

Rennie gave all the information he had to the War Office upon his return, but the War Office felt unable to give out the news of my father's death to anyone, as they felt that they had insufficient evidence for it. Major Rennie initially could not bring himself to tell Granny Grant Duff that he had heard her son had died. He had not been on the spot but with General Fortune at St. Valery. However, Lieutenant Colonel Alwyn V. Holt of the Black Watch felt such deep sorrow for my grandmother's acute anguish that he wrote to her on 12 August from the Queen's Barracks in Perth, saying that Rennie was quite sure my father had been killed by a bullet from a machine gun on the last day of fighting and that 19-year-old Second Lieutenant Alistair Telfer-Smollett had also been killed, by a mortar bomb. Otherwise, there were no other officer casualties. Rennie had no further details, such as the place of burial.

Granny was, of course, frantic, and on 14 August wrote to my mother enclosing a copy of Colonel Holt's letter. Holt assured Granny that 'the Germans [at St. Valery] were treating our wounded and dead with every consideration', but he could add nothing about burials. Granny promised to let my mother know as soon as she received an official notification from the War Office. She added in her letter that she still 'hoped against hope', as I think she did for the rest of her life.[4]

Rennie himself then wrote to Granny on 17 August when he discovered that the War Office was still hesitating to let relations know of a death that was officially unconfirmed. He refers to my father as 'Adrian' and says that as a 'supplementary reservist' he, Rennie, and others in the regiment had liked and admired him and were so delighted to get him back again when the war started.

Thus, my father's death was most reluctantly, and only unofficially, confirmed through fellow officers two months after the fact. The definitive confirmation did not come until much later, with a compassionate letter from Major General Victor Fortune, addressed to 'Mrs Grant Duff' (Granny), dated 7 November and sent from his prison camp.

The absence of any official news about my father from the War Office, even in late August, was shattering for Granny, and my mother, in Canada, must have felt completely numb. Granny wrote to General Telfer-Smollett, father of Alistair, whom Rennie believed had been killed with my father. She also wrote to Guy Campbell, the father of David, another fellow officer, asking for news. She was desperate and sent the letters with stamped envelopes for their replies.

She promised my mother not to put anything about my father's death in *The Times* until she heard from the War Office. She next wrote to the International Red Cross in Geneva, having heard nothing from General Telfer-Smollett or Guy Campbell. It was now 29 August. She finally received an answer from Guy Campbell on 1 September: he was trying to get a message through to David in his prison camp for news of my father. He noted how much David admired and loved my father as a man and a soldier. He added that General Telfer-Smollett had not answered her letter because he had no news of his son (later confirmed to have been killed with my father at Houdetot). Granny received a further letter from General Fortune's wife, Eleanor, encouraging her to write to her husband for news but reiterating that Major Rennie's report must be true, although other prisoners, presumed dead, had suddenly come to light – including a Nigel Courage, for whom a memorial service had already mistakenly taken place. She also suggested that my grandmother write to Colonel Honeyman (who was commanding the Black Watch at the time of my father's death) and gave his prison camp address. She added that postcards were now getting past the censors much faster than letters, so Granny followed her recommendation and switched to postcards. (Consequently, the need to write much in a small space has made her postcards very difficult to read.)

In September 1940, Granny wrote about the distracting and continuous bombing raids and the noise, and how the safest way to get around was by Green Line buses when dashing to High Elms to see her distraught mother or to Oxford to see Shiela.

In a letter of 9 September, Granny explained to my mother that each prisoner of war was allowed to write three letters and three postcards a month and that the correspondence could take six weeks to travel each way, meaning a three-month wait for an answer. Messages through others were a better way forward, but there was still no word from General Telfer-Smollett. In a letter dated 11 September, she expressed a continued hope that my father had been hidden away with 'French people'. On 16 September, she wrote that David Campbell's prison camp address in Germany had been published in the Personal column of *The Times*. On the 17th, she described how the RAF had shot down 185 German 'machines' over Britain the day before and described again the noise of the war in the air and air raid sirens continually going on and off. She talked of a wall of sandbags in the garden at Mulberry Walk. On the 18th, she wrote to say that she was going to her sister-in-law Adelaide Lubbock's refugee hospital to offer help. She added that they must need even grandmothers' help now for the war effort! A postcard sent to my mother on 20 September (my brother Adrian's birthday) said that Mulberry Walk had been badly bombed during the night, but, mercifully, Granny had been staying in Oxford with Shiela. Shiela's Czech friends (Hubert and Naomi Ripka), guests at Mulberry Walk, had already moved to the Cumberland Hotel, whose deep basement offered more protection from bombing. However, her letter of 22 September records that they had been bombed out of the Cumberland and were now at the Ritz! She added that she had spoken to Granny Chance (my mother's mother), then living with her father at Rougham Hall, which had also just been bombed.

There is a long pause in the flow of letters to my mother at this point: the next is dated 4 November 1940 and is a copy of a postcard from Colonel Honeyman written from his prison camp, addressed to 'Alwyn V. Holt, The Black Watch, Perth', dated 16 July. The postcard reconfirmed what everyone had feared: that my father had been killed along with Alistair Telfer-Smollett and Padre Garden in a last stand at Houdetot. This was followed by a copy of a 7 November letter from General Fortune, mentioned above, which also confirmed my father's death. Opened by the censor, and strangely singed around its edges, it was sent from Oflag VII-C/Z, Laufen Castle, Bavaria, where many British soldiers had been imprisoned. It reads: 'By permission of the German authorities, I have been allowed to write you a special letter......I fear there is no doubt about Neill. He was killed on the morning of June 12.....'

General Fortune's letter went on to describe my father's death at Houdetot, while leading his company to a new position to confront the enemy, who 'were threatening to outflank the rest of the battalion'. His body had been identified by David Campbell, who added a line of sympathy at the bottom of the letter. It is a very touching, personal letter, and it states how proud the Regiment was of my father's father, Adrian Grant Duff, who had died leading the 42nd in 1914, and, twenty-six years later, his son, who also died leading his Company of the 42nd.[5]

Fortune, who had fought alongside her husband Adrian in the First World War, had always kept in touch with Granny Grant Duff. He recalled meeting my father as a small boy, tucked up in bed, when on leave in 1916 or 1917. There is also a prison postcard dated 19 November from Colonel Honeyman to Granny, saying how popular Neill was with all ranks and how keenly his death was felt.

David Campbell wrote to my mother from the same prison camp on 10

December 1940, and to Granny Grant Duff on a separate postcard, telling them that he was close beside my father, who was leading the company when he was shot from a tank and killed instantly.

On 18 December 1940, six months after my father was killed, obituaries and personal tributes – including a very moving one from Uncle Peter – finally appeared in *The Times*.

The letter trail then disappears until 4 September 1942, when a very impersonal typed letter from the War Office arrived, stating that Captain N.A.M. Grant Duff, the Black Watch, was buried in Houdetot Communal Cemetery, about fifteen miles southwest of Dieppe. In a letter dated 9 September, Granny was told the War Office could do nothing about verifying the grave, as it was in enemy-occupied territory. However, it was understood that local villagers had been looking after the British graves in France and Belgium. She had waited two years for this trickle of information and was destined to wait another four before she found his place of burial.

On 4 January 1944, Granny received another letter from Eleanor Fortune, telling her that David Campbell had been repatriated thanks to the Red Cross. (He told me that he had feigned complete deafness, and the German prison guards, fed up with him, had asked for his transfer). David went to see Granny as soon as he was back in England but he brought no further news. General Fortune could also have got home through the Red Cross but he refused, saying, 'I brought out the 51st Division and I intend to take them back.'

Granny explored every avenue in her desperate search for my father's grave, particularly once the war came to an end. The next surviving letter regarding the location of the grave is dated 5 June 1946, from David Campbell to Granny. In it, David says he wonders 'if it is in the orchard where we were or moved to the village cemetery'. He describes exactly where they had been when Neill was killed: 'We were down a lane off the main road – on the left coming from St. Valery and there were high trees all along the hedgerows and fields of corn all round: there was a farm house (very small) as well in the field – I wonder if it's there.' He is, of course, referring to the environs of Houdetot.

My grandmother had been communicating after the end of the war with the mayor of Houdetot because he was responsible for the burial of the soldiers killed in his village. It was thanks to him, and my grandmother's utter determination to find the body, that a great mistake came to light. Granny had travelled through the war-ravaged French countryside to Houdetot on 4 June 1946 in search of my father's grave but his name did not appear on any grave in the village cemetery. There were five *inconnus*, the *gardien* told her, when the bodies were exhumed in his presence in 1941 or 1942 (no one could remember the exact date but the Germans were in charge at that time and no records were kept). Two were identified as Hamilton and Smith, and the other three were reburied as *inconnus*. Granny assumed that my father must be one of the *inconnus*, so she went to look for 'M. le Maire', whom she described as 'old, simple, kindly and very poor and asleep on the kitchen table'. He confirmed everything that Granny had been told and sent his daughter to *la mairie* to fetch letters found in the soldiers' pockets. There was nothing to or from my father, but the mayor's wife then produced a notebook in which she had labelled a separate page for each of the *inconnus*, recording what she had found in their pockets before reburial. One page recorded the address of a 'Dr. Hamilton Turner, 77 Cadogan Place, SW1, Lettre 16 Sep 39, Dear M Grant Duff Grande Capitaine'. Returning to the cemetery, Granny looked once more at the rudimentary crosses, one of which was actually inscribed with the name of 'Cap De Hamilton'.

On the sad drive back to Dieppe, it suddenly flashed across Granny's mind that Hamilton Turner's name could be on her son's grave. She rushed to the telephone book as soon as she reached London. Dr Claude Hamilton Turner was still listed at the address written down in the notebook, so Granny dashed off another of her famous letters. On 10 June she received an answer from Hamilton Turner saying that he was very much alive. My father had been buried under the name of this friend, who had written to him quite some time before his death. A fragment of his letter, probably kept by my father for the address, had been found in my father's pocket when he was reburied.

It was now imperative to verify the true identity of the grave with the War Office as soon as possible. Granny wrote to the *maire* at Houdetot on 13 June 1946 to ask if he could let her have the Hamilton Turner letter found with the body. The *maire* replied that the Germans had made them rebury the body with the letter and the money that was also found in the pocket. Hamilton Turner offered to help convince the War Office of the mistaken identity. This evidence for the whereabouts of my father's grave came six years after his death, almost to the day. My poor Granny and my poor mother – what a prolonged and heartrending quest.

Finally, on 15 October 1946, Granny received an official letter from the War Office stating that Captain N.A.M. Grant Duff, the Black Watch, was registered by the Graves Registration Service at the Houdetot Communal

Cemetery. Granny wrote back the following day, on the reverse side of the letter (probably a copy to send to my mother and not to send to the War Office), 'the family and I hope that it will be left there and on no account moved without consultation with us beforehand'.

Sadly, my mother, although she had chosen the inscription for my father's grave, did not have an opportunity to visit it until we went back to England in the summer of 1951. Granny arranged to take her while we children were staying with our other grandmother. It never occurred to me to think that we should have been asked as well – it was their special pilgrimage.

1: Clement Attlee, future Labour Prime Minister, was then Leader of the Opposition in Parliament.

2: Letter from Ursula Grant Duff to Bronio Malinowski dated 18 April 1940.

3: Aunt Lulu's diary: 'On 27th May the evacuation of Dunkirk begins, on 28th May Belgium surrenders, on 1st June the family hears that Neill is no longer with the B.E.F., on 4th June the evacuation of Dunkirk is completed and on 12th June Neill's First Battalion Black Watch and the 51st Highland Division surrender at Saint Valery en Caux in Normandy. Neill is assumed to have been taken prisoner.'

4: My mother's brother Peter wrote to my mother on 15 August when he heard the news and reminded her that it was only a year earlier that they had all been together at Rougham for the weekend, and on the Monday breakfast train that they had said, 'Although the news looks pretty bad – but still we cannot go to war – there must be a way out somewhere', and now that life had gone forever. He added that my mother had been so wise to take her children to Canada as the raids on London were intensifying seriously.

5: It was unusual in the Black Watch to send the son to the Front Line if the father had been killed in the First World War. Did Neill insist on going? Today, Winston Churchill is criticised for the 'sacrifice' of the 51st Highland Division (see, for instance, Saul David, *Churchill's Sacrifice of the Highland Division: France 1940*, Brassey's, 1994). He had decided they must stay in northern France, at any cost, to support the French army against the German advance and a potential invasion of Britain.

CHAPTER 8

Refugees in Canada

Granny Chance, with whom we had spent much of the summer of 1939 at Rougham, had been very keen that we should continue to stay there for the duration of the war. She thought it would be perfectly safe, buried as it was in the depths of the country. However, she was badly mistaken. RAF ammunition was buried in all the home woods and suspicious characters were discovered trespassing. It is possible that the German intelligence believed that the RAF Command was occupying Rougham. On 23 September 1940, the tenth day of the Blitz, a bomb fell directly through the centre of the house. Fortunately, there were few staff present, as most of them were at the Front or away for the weekend. My grandmother and great-grandfather were both in the house and had to be rescued by the RAF, who were indeed billeted nearby. My great-grandfather's famous mezzotint collection, which hung in the dining room, was completely destroyed. His memory never returned after that night. He had created a gentleman's country house life for his wife and children in 1904 and only thirty-six years later this life had been rudely swept away forever.

Granny Chance recounted the blast to me many years later. She was so terrified that she clung to the bedpost with all her might until rescued by an airman climbing through the window of the tower where she slept. The head housemaid, Alice Currey, told me years later that when the airman reappeared on his ladder carrying my grandmother, she was smothered from head to toe in soot from the fireplace in her room. As she was always very elegant, this sight shocked all those present!

On 10 June 1940, with no knowledge of what was happening to my father, my mother informed me that we were going to Canada. I was four and a half and had never been anywhere except to see my great-grandparents and to the Isle of Wight with a bucket and spade. The prospect of an invasion of Britain was on everyone's mind, and no time was lost in buying tickets and getting passports. We sailed from Liverpool on RMS *Scythia* on 25 June 1940. The family knew by this time that my father had been reported missing.

Barbara and Lulu in Bath, before the war, 1934/5

Both my grandmothers, a number of aunts, and a few older uncles, saw us off at Euston Station. There were masses of other women and children, the latter all carrying, like myself, teddy bears and gas masks. Granny Grant Duff pressed into my hand her gold watch and told me to give it to my mother on the journey, as she was bound to be short of money. I realised that this was a serious commission, and that everyone was very upset.

On the ship we were a party of eleven people, including one of my father's older sisters, Aunt Lulu, and three young boys, as well as two teenage Lubbock cousins, Eric and Olivia. Their family's lovely old nurse, Nan Wrigley, who

I remember had intense blue eyes, looked after us all when the disgruntled governess, Miss Potts, retired to her cabin with seasickness.

I remember nothing of Liverpool but, according to Aunt Lulu's diary, we were on the ship for lunch and it moved off the quay at 2.20pm. For a whole day, we waited in the mouth of the Mersey and actually set out to sea on 27 June. The reason for the delay might have been bad weather or concern about German U-boats. The voyage left an indelible impression on me.

On board the *Scythia*: (l-r) Alex Boyle, Olivia Lubbock, Richard Boyle, Flavia, Adrian, Barbara and Anthony Boyle

Once underway, we had to wear our life jackets at all times, and this meant squashing past each other in narrow corridors below deck. We slept in a tiny cabin. I was very irritated because my mother, whom I barely knew, spent most of her time attending to a little girl of six who had joined us – the daughter of family friends. Aunt Lulu's diary describes how seasick we all were and how rough and cold the crossing was. Fog delayed our arrival in Halifax, Nova Scotia, by a whole day. We finally docked on 6 July at Pier 21. This pier still bears a plaque to commemorate the arrival in Canada of approximately one million immigrants between 1928 and 1971. Once through customs and immigration, apparently expedited by my brother Adrian's persistent screaming, we boarded a special boat train travelling via Quebec to Montreal, where we changed for

Toronto. My mother once told me that she and Aunt Lulu had eaten only bread on this train journey, as they were so short of money for food for all of us.

On our arrival in Toronto, we all tumbled out of the train to be greeted by a very welcoming but very dismayed Canadian couple, Aileen and Doug Woods, friends of my father's Uncle Maurice whom my mother had met at High Elms some years before.[1] They had agreed to sponsor Maurice's children, Eric and Olivia Lubbock, aged 12 and 14, respectively. The censored telegram from London had implied that only these two were arriving. However, we were not to know this until later, when some of us were parceled out to other friends for the night. I recall being allowed to sit up late and play with someone's beautiful dollhouse. The dolls even had toothbrushes.

The situation was grave. We had to be housed somewhere for the foreseeable future. My mother and Aunt Lulu went immediately to the Brantford Centre of the Eugenics Society in Toronto, seeking help organised by Granny Grant Duff. However, it appears that they were so shocked by the Society's support of birth control that they did not wish to be involved in any way! Luckily, a very large and magical family house, 'Anneville', was then offered by the Woods's cousins, the Walkers, and we moved in on 9 July. It was out in the country, about seventy miles east of Toronto, and without electric light, refrigeration or domestic help of any kind. My mother had never cooked a meal, trimmed a gas lamp or looked after children. Luckily, Aunt Lulu was much more practical, and experienced with children, so they coped. We were all survivors and we loved our new home, where the sun shone on a huge garden with lily ponds and a trout stream. There was also a swimming pool filled with green water and a lot of jumping frogs. We were given the services of a 'manservant', as my mother called him (actually the caretaker of the property), called Vernon, who was always in a straw hat even in the house. He helped with the shopping, fetched large blocks from the ice house to refrigerate the fresh food, and drove my mother and Aunt Lulu whenever they needed to go outside the property.

My mother wrote to her brother Peter on 28 July to say we had left England in such a rush that she had posted her farewell letter to him unaddressed! She gives the impression of liking Canada and says she will have to start life afresh somewhere after the blow about my father. She obviously had not held out any hope of his still being alive – long before she received the War Office telegram. She voices her uncertainty of future plans for the winter months, and of possibly being separated from Aunt Lulu. She says she could go out to the west and stay with their cousin Brian Chance – but without much enthusiasm. She speaks of memories of Rougham from their childhood and says it would be the place she would miss most in England.

As the summer wore on, I did get to know my mother better and finally understood in my remote and childish manner that she was very unhappy. I remember the day she received the telegram from Granny Grant Duff (dated 12 July, only three days after our arrival at Anneville), confirming that my father was believed missing. She and I and my brother Adrian were sitting in the garden on a rug, and she was crying. I just felt completely inadequate. The distance between us never really narrowed from that moment onwards. I think my brother gave her much greater comfort, although he was only eighteen months at the time. In letters to her mother, Aunt Lulu observed that my mother was fairly easy to live with but very reserved. I suspect my mother almost resented the very active role Granny took in trying to find out what had happened to my father; it was almost as if Granny had taken over my mother's role.

The tragedy of my father's death sealed our fate. The Dick family, business friends of the Woods's in Toronto, lent all of us a large, centrally heated cottage for the winter in the nearby town of Cobourg, where they lived. However, my mother did try striking out on her own in the spring of 1941. She travelled by train with my brother and me across Canada to Kamloops in British Columbia. I remember little about the three-day journey except my disappointment over the porters. My mother had explained to me that they would be 'coloured', so I was expecting red, blue and green porters rather than only black.

My mother's first cousin, Brian Chance, was manager of the ranch on Douglas Lake where we stayed, well away from civilisation. He had been in love with my mother since meeting her at an earlier stage in England. My mother was apparently the only 'white woman' in a thirty-mile radius and attracted much attention. On Saturday nights, the local Canadian Indians would gallop through the woods on horseback with flaming torches. Initially, my mother went out riding alone but Cousin Brian wisely discouraged her, in favour of fishing with the blacksmith on the lake. I was made to join these boring fishing trips as a sort of chaperone and had to sit firmly between them in the middle of the boat! On another occasion, I accompanied Brian in his truck to visit an 'Indian reserve' for lunch. I found the meat tough and distasteful and the children dirty and smelly. I would not stand next to them to have my photograph taken! It was arrogant of me, but I was unhappy and out of my depth.

Flavia with Canadian Indian children, 1941

Another day, my mother lost a very beautiful, tiny pocket watch given to her by my father. It was covered with lizard skin and pulled in and out of its cover to show you the time. She had dropped it in the long grass near the main ranch house. All the ranch hands were summoned out to look for it but, alas, it was to no avail. My mother was terribly upset. The ranch was a strange adventure altogether, and we returned in July to the tranquility and comfort of Anneville and the companionship of the Boyle cousins (Richard, Anthony and Ursula, Aunt Lulu's children).

When Aunt Lulu and the cousins returned to England in 1943, due to encouraging news from the Front, my mother decided to stay on in Cobourg. I felt very sad as their car pulled away from the kerb of the Dicks' wooden frame cottage where we had spent so much time together. Happily, we were able to rekindle our comradeship in later life.

My mother could not talk about our father or the circumstances of his death, and we were not allowed to mention England or any desire to return to it. We were to be 'Canadians' from now on. The ban was only partially raised when Granny Chance, my mother's mother, managed to come and see us in 1947 and 1948, travelling on a small freighter bound for Montreal. She came with delicious English chocolate and piles of white linen handkerchiefs, and wore elegant pre-war tweed suits and intoxicating scent. She also smoked flat Turkish cigarettes after dinner in an elegant cigarette holder. For years, she represented for me the very essence of my homeland.

Granny Chance with my stepfather (r), in a Montreal restaurant feeding a piglet, 1948

The great attraction of Cobourg, where we now lived, seventy miles east of Toronto on Lake Ontario, was the elite, old-fashioned American summer community. These rich and well-travelled people arrived in their straw boaters, drank highballs of whiskey and soda before lunch, and were waited on by the black domestic servants they brought with them. They were the sophisticated descendants of the iron and steel barons of Pittsburgh, intellectuals from New York, or softly spoken southerners from Kentucky, and they had all been to Europe. Before the years of high taxation in the Twenties and Thirties, they had discovered Cobourg and had built themselves large colonial-style houses, always painted white, with lovely lawns and magnificent flower beds stretching at least half a mile down to the shores of Lake Ontario. They were very charming and kind and cheered my mother up. She learned to drink dry martinis at the constant round of dinner parties – parties which continued in a modified version even after the Americans joined the war.

Unfortunately, the flow of dry martinis brought more tragedy. The extraordinarily handsome young Adonis who made the best cocktails at these parties, the Dicks' son David, became our stepfather in 1945. He had everything going for him – charm, wit and intelligence – and was a strong swimmer and skier, but, unknown to my mother, he had been attending sophisticated adult parties since the age of fourteen, disguising his shyness with those lethal drinks. Within a year of their marriage, it became clear that he was a miserable and incurable alcoholic. He could not work, and we were always short of money. The fear of no money stayed with me for years – I even worried that my mother would not be able to afford a proper wedding, if I ever got to that point. Our family in England was desperate with worry and tried to get all of us – or at least Adrian and me – back to England, but to no avail. My half-brother, also named David, was born at the end of 1945, but this seemed to exacerbate the situation. My stepfather was always jealous of his son. We lived a curious sort of prison existence. Life at school was a relief from the tension and loneliness of home. Now we had two fathers whom we could never mention to outsiders! When questioned about our stepfather, we were trained to say that he was ill, and no more. Our mother decided to become a Roman Catholic for solace and

David Dick, my half-brother, aged 5,
in the woods at Banff, Alberta

Adrian in the Canadian Rockies

support, but this produced more angst, as she spent what little time we had together trying to convince us to join a religion that seemed to be destroying our stepfather's family with a burden of hidden shame. When we went back to England for the Festival of Britain in the summer of 1951, the English relations tried to persuade our mother to ask for a legal separation but she would not. Her refusal to leave our stepfather contributed to a rift between herself and her children, and to our half-brother's lifelong mental health problems.

Without the glamorous summer visitors, Cobourg proved to be a very dull and provincial Canadian town like so many others strung along the lakeshore between Toronto and Montreal. However, I loved the beauty of northern Ontario; Georgian Bay had been made famous by the Group of Seven painters. Nevertheless, Ontario was completely overshadowed by the breathtaking Canadian Rockies. We moved to these mountains when I was nearly fourteen, and Adrian eleven, with the hope of a permanent cure for my stepfather. We lived in Banff, at the centre of a huge National Park where we were surrounded by wild animals. We would meet vicious moose on the walk to school, which we were warned to keep clear of, as well as small herds of more friendly elk. Red deer would come looking in full rubbish bins by moonlight and fly gracefully over the fences if disturbed. Black bears prowled around the outskirts of the town, and very large and dangerous grizzly bears roamed in the forest.

We arrived in early January 1950, in sixty-degree-below-zero temperatures, and hastily discarded urban winter clothes for full skiing outfits, Indian socks and moccasins so light that one felt one was running barefoot when wearing them. Our mother had no understanding of the cold, and our faces ached with frostbite. We had to keep the taps running constantly so the pipes would not freeze. However, although we did not learn much at the local school, we skied and skied, and in the spring and summer we explored glacier-fed lakes and towering mountain peaks. At last I understood what beauty really meant.

Sadly, nothing of this great adventure provided relief for my stepfather, and we were obliged to return to the monotony of Cobourg life. We spent many hours helping our mother heave and haul our drunken stepfather upstairs and into bed, but the subject was never discussed. I was sent to board at Havergal College, School for Young Ladies in Toronto, which allowed me an escape. From there, I aimed to get into McGill University in Montreal. Adrian also went to boarding school, and then to the University of New Brunswick. He and I lost touch almost completely during the last years of our childhood.

The only rewarding event of our late childhood was our trip to England for most of the summer of 1951 – the year of the Festival of Britain, when the British people really saw hope for the future. Rationing was still in place, but our coupons helped friends and family to obtain more meat, butter and sugar, so we were popular guests. On the train from Liverpool to London we were enchanted by the separate compartments and the dining coach with proper tables. In the latter, the windows were wide open and the waiters, in white jackets, would dust the smuts off the Dover sole with linen napkins. Cheap and plentiful Dover sole and cold ham were the only choices on any menu in those days. Brown Windsor soup came first, and trifle for pudding.

We spent a lot of time with my mother's mother, Granny Chance, at Field House near Thurston in Suffolk, not far from the ruins of Rougham, and almost an equal amount with Granny Grant Duff, my father's mother, in London. Each was very jealous of time spent with the other. However, we found their lifestyles refreshingly different. At Field House, a large thatched cottage, we were surrounded by sweet-smelling roses, bowls of succulent strawberries and lavender fresh from the garden. In town, the emphasis was on meeting all those people who had known our father, and sardines on toast were the usual fare.

During one of our stays at Field House that summer, but unknown to us at the time, our mother went to France with Granny Grant Duff to see our father's grave at Houdetot. She never told us where she had been and never went again.

As with every event connected with our father's death, it was carefully hidden away in a secret compartment of her mind.

Two years later, I left Havergal and moved on to McGill University in Montreal. My mother was so pleased that she had managed to save enough money (inherited from my father) to send me to university; she had longed to have this opportunity for herself. Where she misjudged the situation, however, was in following too closely the Dick family's advice. They insisted I should leave school a year early 'to get out of black stockings' and meet the opposite sex. This advice was no doubt motivated by the idea of a good marriage being the only future for a woman! I was not ready for this move. I had been elected Head of my House at Havergal, a great honour, and I would have been better prepared for university by the more rigorous standard of teaching in the 6th Form. I had little choice in the matter, but I have regretted the Dick family's influence on this decision ever since.

While I was at McGill University, I returned to Banff with friends to do a summer holiday job as a dining room cashier in the fashionable Banff Springs Hotel. Staff were given a consecutive day and a half off per week and were allowed to use the pools and the golf course on those days. For most of us, however, the call of the wild was much more appealing, and we organised trips to climb mountains and explore hidden lakes. I was very keen on this challenge, but my last adventure was almost a disaster. I planned to walk into the forest with two companions to find Emerald Lake, famed for its breathtaking setting and extraordinarily rich colour. We had been informed that there was a log cabin for overnight hikers, stocked with emergency rations and thick blankets. To begin our trek, we had to persuade someone working on the new Trans-Canada Highway to drive us to the point closest to the lake, because there was no access road. This was strictly illegal, so we decided not to sign out with the wardens at Banff National Park. We were duly dropped off and, in the evening sun, found our way to the lake with the help of a map. It was grizzly bear country, and we kept seeing their huge tracks in the soft earth. After a dinner of sirloin steak, carried in our knapsacks, we slept well, and the next morning we set off early to enjoy the beauty of the lake and to find another trail home. As dusk fell, we were still searching in vain for the path, so we decided to sleep in the woods and get up at first light to carry on. We had foolishly forgotten to bring a compass but thought we could be guided by the sun, as we had no idea where we were on the map. We awoke at dawn to find a large moose more or less standing over our bodies, which were huddled together against the extreme cold. I remember thinking we must get up immediately and keep walking, although which way, and for how long, I had no idea. It made me realise how people can get lost forever – depression and fear make one feel there is no point in continuing. We passed a trapper's cabin but saw no sign of recent use. In the afternoon we found a path, which appeared to have some sense of purpose as it opened up before us. We followed it. At about five o'clock we finally burst into the open and were confronted by the mighty Bow River with its dangerously strong current, apparently an impassable barrier between us and a distant section of lonely highway. No amount of shouting was going to carry our voices over the roar of the water. Evidently, wading through the rushing torrent was our only hope of salvation. We put our watches between our teeth and our cameras and boots round our necks, linked arms in a death grip and slowly forded the rushing current. We were fools, but we made it! Our clothes were soaked and our pockets crammed with silt from the force of the glacial water. We staggered up to the edge of the road and feebly tried to hitch a lift. A few vehicles passed us by but, finally, the driver of a small open truck stopped for us, horrified at our bedraggled state. He generously drove us the long journey back to the Banff Springs Hotel. We had walked miles off course in the wrong direction, and were to be in acute trouble for not registering our trip. We were fined, a large sum of money to us, and were lucky not to have been dismissed by the Hotel. The Chief Warden did relent slightly, in his miniature courtroom, and admitted that had we been missing for a second night, they would have been obliged to come and look for us by helicopter. Needless to say, our last few days off were spent quietly – on the golf course.

1: cf. letter to her brother Peter Chance 28 July 1940.

CHAPTER 9

In France with Granny Grant Duff

When I reached the age of eighteen, rescue came in sight. I went back to England in the summer, for the second time, to stay with all my blood relations. This time I was more or less grown up, and free to choose my invitations. I went to France with Granny Grant Duff to see my father's grave. We had an enchanting passage across the English Channel, sitting on the sunlit open deck of a Channel steamer bound for Dieppe, and, once there, we installed ourselves in a wonderful old inn called La Sole Dieppoise. The dining room was filled with the aroma of Camembert and overripe pears, and the only guest lavatory was halfway up the curving staircase to the bedrooms. I vaguely wondered how my grandmother dealt with this bizarre set-up, although she said of the bidets in the bedrooms that 'they did make possible, washing the impossible'.

The following morning we were driven to the tiny village of Houdetot where my father is buried. The mayor's wife, whom Granny had known for years, came with us to see the six graves in a corner of the village churchyard. She had been present at the original burial of these soldiers. This lady related that after a night in her barn at Houdetot, the small detachment of Black Watch officers and soldiers had set off again to confront the German advance. She had not dared to keep them hidden after daybreak.

My grandmother spoke fluent French, and we lunched with the mayor's whole family in their seventeenth-century farmhouse with the chickens wandering in and out over the flagstone floor. I was encouraged to drink Calvados by the old mayor, which filled my grandmother with alarm.

Upon our return to Dieppe, she suggested that we have a cup of tea in an open-air café looking out over the sea. It was another lovely afternoon, and I was enjoying the crowd of passersby. Suddenly, she turned to me and said, 'I come here on these trips as I always hope that perhaps one day I will see your father pass by in his French beret.' I was shaken; only then did I fully understand how cruel the war had been for her and for my mother. Granny, exhausted, went to bed very early, leaving me to my own devices.

I lay awake all night on my bed, fully dressed and rigid with fear: I had not realised that grief could take such a sinister form and induce such false hope, almost hallucination.

The rest of the French trip was sheer joy. We had lunch in Rouen with old friends of Granny's and explored the beautiful cathedral. We took the train to Paris and stayed at the Hotel Gard du Nord and ate in a local buffet, as my grandmother did not believe in spending precious pennies on expensive hotels and food. The following morning, we took a taxi to the Louvre to see what Granny considered the four most important works of art: the *Mona Lisa*, the *Winged Victory of Samothrace*, the *Venus de Milo* and the Marie de' Medici cycle of paintings by Rubens. We took another taxi to lunch with Clare de Loriol, daughter of my grandfather Adrian's sister Tiny, who worked at UNESCO and lived with a very friendly and very masculine American lady. They had a lovely flat looking out over the Eiffel Tower. Lunch was delicious, although I had never seen a whole boiled artichoke before and did not know how to eat it! Yet another taxi swept us on that afternoon to Les Invalides to see Napoleon's tomb. Granny always engaged the driver in deep conversation in fluent French, asking about the political situation and about his family. The evening was spent at Les Folies Bergère. This had been suggested by the ticket seller at the box office of the Comédie-Française, which was unfortunately closed in August. It was great fun to go with my sparkling grandmother. Her eyes were transfixed as nude after nude appeared at the top of a splashing waterfall on stage, or swinging above the heads of the audience in a gilded birdcage. Neither Fragonard nor Boucher could have done better. My mother, when told, was horrified and made me promise not to tell Granny Chance I had been to such an event. In earlier times, my mother explained, English ladies were not invited to the 'Follies' but left to spend a quiet evening in the hotel. However, Granny Grant Duff was prepared to embrace any new experience to give pleasure to her 'Canadian' granddaughter, as she put it. After our return to London the following evening, she greeted me in a large white bath towel and said, with peals of laughter, 'I feel quite decent after seeing those ladies at the Folies Bergère!'

A return to Canada in the autumn of 1954 was imperative, as I had three more years of McGill ahead of me. However, my plans were firmly made and all that remained was to save enough money to return to London upon completion of my degree. I never wanted to see Canada again. The person who supported this decision most openly and most wholeheartedly was my mother's brother, Uncle Peter. He had been at Christie's ever since leaving Eton and adored the

Uncle Peter at Christie's *c.* 1958

art world and travelling in Europe. On our first trip back to England in the summer of 1951, he had taken me to the Wallace Collection with my rather reluctant brother and talked us through every room. I have such a clear memory of his passion, whether he was pointing out an eighteenth-century French chair, a *boule armoire* or a Reynolds portrait. I was literally enchanted. He was to be a formative influence on me.

Uncle Peter later became a sort of surrogate father, and I came to understand how like him I was in many ways. If you are removed from your extended family and your own country at an early age, you cannot properly identify yourself – or perhaps I could not because I was neither like my mother nor what she had hoped for in a daughter.

When I was still quite young, my mother regularly received forms from Burke's Peerage. However, in middle life she rebelled against the whole idea of the British aristocracy or ruling class and firmly threw all the forms into the wastepaper basket. She explained to me that 'life is not about who you are but what you personally make of it'. I was secretly very disappointed, as I longed to be 'someone' and go back to England to be reunited with my family on both sides. I did not have seventy-one first cousins like Granny Grant Duff but I still had a sufficient number to make a large group of friends. I had to wait until I was twenty-two years old to escape from Canada and remake a life in England.

CHAPTER 10

The Return of the Native

I left Canada forever in April 1959. A first fling of that summer was on a Sunday evening when Uncle Peter and Aunt Paddy took me with them to dine with the Birches, very close friends of theirs. The Birches lived in a large house on Prince Albert Terrace, facing Regent's Park. I thought these friends the most exotic people I had ever met and longed not to be dressed in a conventional flowered cotton frock from Liberty's. Simon was plump and jolly and dressed in a red velvet smoking jacket, Bettine in a black dress with a skirt that swirled round her as she moved. We drank champagne and danced to music from the film *Gigi* (a recent winner in the Academy awards), music which at that time was playing on every gramophone in London. They were all enthusiastic about my forthcoming trip to Europe, full of advice about what to see and, most especially, what to eat. My total lack of sophistication must have been painful for them.

This two-month trip, with two friends from McGill, began well, with plans, I thought, to explore every church and every gallery. I had not realised that my friends were more interested in the cafés and the beaches, and we nearly split up for good in Madrid. I was further handicapped for much of the time, as a few days later, in Seville, I fell and broke a bone in my foot. I was forced to see the rest of Spain, and most of Italy, in plaster to the knee. I could not believe my bad luck. At times, it was to my advantage: in Rome, for the glorious celebrations on the Feast of Saint Peter and Saint Paul, I was virtually lifted over the heads of the faithful in St Peter's and given a prime seat with the nuns in the choir facing Bernini's famous high altar. It gave me a magnificent view of that charismatic figure, Pope John XXIII, smothered in lace and wreathed in smiles. He was swept into the vast basilica on a gilded papal throne above the heads of thousands of exuberant pilgrims, a thrilling experience soon to be discarded by Pope Paul VI as extravagant pomp and ceremony, and undemocratic.

The plaster cast was finally removed in Venice. My chastened friends, who had been obliged to look after me all this time, were now converted and happy to follow me around the myriad churches in that city.

The summer ended in a pilgrimage to Scotland. I was taken to the Black Watch Museum at Perth by Scottish cousins of my stepfather's and then put on a bus for the Highlands, in the pouring rain, clutching a bottle of whiskey for my father's great friend, David Campbell. I was quite nervous. I only knew him as the last person to have seen my father before he died.

David had kept in touch with Aunt Shiela after Granny Grant Duff's death earlier that year, and it was her idea that I should go and stay with him on Loch Fyne in Argyllshire. He was a confirmed bachelor, having found marriage impossible after only three weeks. He wore a kilt and a tam o'shanter. He was very friendly and jolly but rather at a loss as to how to treat the unsophisticated and relatively foreign grown-up daughter of his dearest friend in the Black Watch. We drove back to his ramshackle farmhouse with glorious evening sunshine illuminating the blue-green surface of the loch. He offered me scrambled eggs for dinner, in a very spartan kitchen, and I produced the bottle of whiskey with some fear and trembling. It broke the ice! Hours later, I went to bed knowing I had a new friend, and understanding so much more about my father. David roared with laughter about how they had swung on the chandelier together in the officers' mess. I was amazed, as I had never had my father presented in this merry and rather wild light before. David also described how the Germans had appeared out of nowhere that June morning in France. He told me my father had been shot and killed from a tank and that he, David, had been taken prisoner and shipped off to a prisoner-of-war camp. He went on to relate that he had tried to make himself very unpopular with the German guards by feigning acute deafness. He had hoped that that this would get him exchanged for a similarly injured German prisoner. On reaching London in 1946, he had gone straight to the War Office and reported what had happened at Houdetot.

Our friendship endured for years, and I invited him to my wedding so that he could see my mother again. I shall never forget how shattered he looked as she fled from the church and how he stumbled over the pew to follow. She could not face him. I was deeply embarrassed and saddened.

This first year back in England was tough, despite the family's support. I had tried so hard to return for Granny Grant Duff but she had died of pneumonia two months before I arrived. I was heartbroken. However, Granny Chance was thrilled to see me and spoil me, and I stayed with her often at Field House. Aunt Lulu and Uncle Robert kept in constant touch, and I stayed with them often at Hermongers Barn, their much-loved house in Sussex.

By autumn, I needed to earn some money. I had been brought up to work, as we never had any money, but was only encouraged to be a receptionist or a shorthand typist, not a professional woman. Marriage and 'being the brains behind your husband's throne' was the family concern. However, I found a job advertised on the front page of *The Times* for an organisation called The Emergency Bed Service, run by a retired naval commander. Working in conjunction with the relatively new National Health Service, it was a 24-hour service for finding hospital beds for critically ill people, particularly on cold, foggy winter nights. A team of twenty-four young women worked on telephones in pairs, and each pair was allocated a specific area of Greater London. Our premises were in an old warehouse near Southwark Bridge. We were trained to identify the symptoms of each patient, learn which symptoms deserved priority and which hospitals were most cooperative. If there was an emergency, four of us might combine forces on four different telephones. It was a very exciting and challenging existence, and my friends and family dined out on the *double entendre* of 'The Emergency Bed Service'!

CHAPTER 11

In Greece and Yugoslavia

Spring 1960 brought the chance to go to Greece and Yugoslavia, so I counted my pennies and decided to resign from my job and seek adventure. In Greece, I stayed with one of the three daughters of Bronio Malinowski, Granny Grant Duff's friend who had been so kind to my mother at the Mulberry Walk dinner parties. Helena and I explored the environs of Athens together. Her mother had lived an invalid's life in the South Tyrol and when she died, Helena and her sisters kept her house. Later I used to stay with her there and go for wonderful walks with her in the mountains. When my husband John started coming, too, she would often talk to him of the virtues of the Austro-Hungarian Empire into which her father had been born. She spoke several languages and was a most amusing and stimulating conversationalist. Helena became a friend for life.

Yugoslavia was a revelation. I knew next to nothing about it except that it was a communist federation governed by Tito. Before leaving for Athens, I had arranged to meet my cousin Anthony Boyle and his wife, Sheila, under the clock at Zagreb Station at 3pm on 1 June. We managed to find each other (although the station did not actually have a clock), and we set off to explore the country in their car with two small ex-army tents borrowed from Uncle Robert. The country was very poor, and I was amazed to see the old men in the villages sitting outside on the steps of their humble cottages, knitting, while the women worked in the fields. This role reversal was not something I had ever experienced.

That summer, the first modern highway was being blasted through the mountains from north to south and we were held up for a whole day, sitting in the car while they worked on the section of road ahead. The unexpected combination of Muslim graveyards at Sarajevo, Roman ruins at Split, and medieval streets in Dubrovnik was largely untouched by modern life. I doubt that the atmosphere was very different from that my parents had experienced travelling through the Balkans in the Thirties. At Sarajevo, we 'camped' in the bridal suite at the Grand Hotel, as our tents were soaked from the endless rain. From the windows, we could see the famous bridge where the Archduke Ferdinand's motor car had made its fatal turn in the summer of 1914.

It was a fairly lonely holiday, as we had no language in common with the local inhabitants, and I have no recollection of crowded streets. One local fellow in Sarajevo took a shine to Anthony and insisted on taking us out to dinner. We used sign language amicably until he got Anthony very drunk on *slivovitz* and we fled. I think he was harmless, but it put us off any more local encounters.

CHAPTER 12

In Egypt

These adventures in southern and eastern Europe brought my indecision about what to do with my life to an end. I was determined to travel further afield despite my awareness that I was not making a niche for myself in Britain, as planned. My wish came true through the unlikely medium of a secretarial college in Queen's Gate. At this forward-looking institution, proper careers for women with accurate typing and shorthand were guaranteed. Although not a star at either, I managed to talk my way into the Foreign Office and was sent, as a secretary, to Brussels, after a month in London learning how to type dispatches. I loved the charm of Bruges and Ghent and weekend trips to northern France, but I found that they did not offset the tedium of typing endless reports about the Belgian Congo. However, the subsequent offer of a post at the embassy in Cairo changed my whole perception of life.

I drove myself from Brussels to Genoa in order to take my treasured Renault Dauphine to Egypt. The military attaché at the embassy insisted on mapping out my route across Europe, selecting picturesque places for me to spend the nights. I drove on my own for three consecutive days with my trunk in the boot. The trunk provided ballast when the winter mistral threatened to blow the car off the road in Provence. Every night I ate a delicious dinner washed down with quantities of red wine.

When we docked at Alexandria, I was met by British embassy staff delivering their diplomatic 'sea bag' to my ship. They drove back to Cairo with me, past the camel trains and through the beautiful green delta. It was February 1961, and this was the only day I wore a winter coat for the next sixteen months.

I was overwhelmed by Egypt's exotic beauty from the moment I arrived. Embassy life here was quite different, much less rigid and formal than in Brussels. One of my fellow secretaries encouraged me to have riding lessons with the head groom of the stables at Giza. After a number of lessons, he and I would gallop across the desert at dusk, flashing past the famous pyramids. On one occasion, he whacked my horse's flank so hard that it ran away with me, giving him the opportunity to ride up alongside and pull me onto his own horse and into his arms, leaving me completely compromised! This particular adventure killed my enthusiasm for any more lessons, and I was aware that there was so much more to experience in this captivating country.

Embassy life was enlivened further by a group of young, adventure-seeking diplomats. Among my favourites were Salman Haidar, Third Secretary at the Indian Embassy, who used to read Shakespeare to me on long, hot afternoons, crouched on the arm of an over-stuffed chair in his flat; and Frank Taylor from the British Council (obliged to pose as a cultural attaché, as the British Council was suspected of harbouring spies), who organised extraordinary expeditions. Both he and Salman had a thorough knowledge of Islamic history and art. I had none, and benefited enormously from their company. They took me several times to a grand town house in medieval Cairo to visit the antiquarian, Yuri Miloslavski. It was another world, as were the city buses crammed with Arabs in shawls and *galabias*, with small boys in striped pyjamas hanging on to the doors and windows for a free ride.

One of Frank's more audacious outings was an evening trip to a celebration in a Sufi village, some way from Cairo. I am not sure that as British Embassy staff we should have been there. Frank made many friends amongst Egyptians I suspect we were not meant to fraternise with. As the night wore on, the chanting and the dancing, lit by flares, became alarmingly wild and I wondered if we would ever see the lights of Cairo again.

In the city itself, Frank organised groups of us to explore the Old City, with its beautiful medieval mosques and Coptic churches. One could never go about alone. These excursions sometimes led to a hasty exodus as we were pelted with hard mud balls by the ragged children in the back streets. They had nothing better to do than torment foreign sightseers and thought it was a great joke when we started to run for safety. The long evenings would be spent at embassy parties or dancing on the roof of the Semiramis Hotel, overlooking the Nile. There were belly dancers to entertain us, and very good food.

However, political clouds were always hovering, and we were constantly reminded of the need for caution. It was only five years since the Suez crisis, which had made the British so unpopular in the international community. A list of Egyptians we were allowed to meet socially was kept in the Chancery offices and this had to be adhered to. Amongst those on the list were a number of rich and charming young men whose families had supported King Farouk. They enjoyed the company of the embassy women as we were emancipated, unlike most Egyptian women at that time. The latter could go to Groppi's, the famous café in central Cairo, for tea or a drink, but they could not spend the weekends camping out on the beaches near El Alamein or on the Red Sea. One evening, a group of us went to the main square near the cathedral and saw Nasser delivering one of his great speeches. The whole space was floodlit, and his head and shoulders were projected onto a large screen in black-and-white film. His eyes shone like headlamps and his teeth flashed and the crowd roared with excitement. Every inch of space was taken up by a male figure; men wearing the long *galabia* and a *tarboosh* and small boys in their habitual pyjamas.

The Anglican cathedral, designed by Adrian Gilbert Scott (grandson of Sir Gilbert Scott), then stood proudly by the Nile; it was demolished a decade after I left, like so many other romantic buildings, to make way for a concrete bridge. Old toppling houses were the order of the day, and a huge stretch of open country lay between the picturesque island of Gezira, with its smart district of Zamalek and the Gezira Sporting Club, and the Great Pyramids of Giza.

Trips to see more distant parts of this thrilling land took up all my spare time. Sometimes Frank's day trips ended in disaster. He was very keen to follow the Baedeker guide, a practice which often led us into military training camps concealed by the sand dunes of the desert. Such mistakes could involve hours of explaining and nervous waiting while the local commander tried to call his superiors in Cairo on an antiquated field telephone. Eventually, we would be released and escorted back to the main road without ever seeing our pyramid!

My first overnight trip was to Mount Sinai via the Suez Canal Zone. This was set up by Egyptian friends. It was a major effort to organise the trip, as we had to take all our own food and drink in ice boxes in a fleet of battered taxis. We needed special visas to enter the Sinai peninsula and, alas, for some unexplained reason, our key Egyptian organiser and friend, Ismail, was forbidden access and sent back. This put a heavy dampener on proceedings, but we finally got to Saint Catherine's Monastery after a day's driving across the desert, including a stop at the alleged site of Moses' 'burning bush'. Suddenly, there was the majestic monastery rising out of the plain. The monks were already dwindling in number and anxious for the revenue we were bringing in. They made us as comfortable as possible and showed us the kitchens. At four in the morning, we were woken by the rhythmic beating of a wooden gong calling the devout to the Angelus. After breakfast we were taken to see the remarkable collection of icons and manuscripts: I am told these are still

Phillip Ward Green and Flavia in the Valley of the Kings, near Luxor

there, despite all the ensuing political upheavals. We hired camels to explore Mount Sinai but walked up to the saint's shrine on Mount Saint Catherine. It was all so beautiful and unspoilt.

On my only trip to Upper Egypt, I travelled with Irene Beeson, a controversial Irish journalist who had lived for years in the Middle East, and Phillip Ward Green, who taught English in Cairo at the smart Egyptian school in Heliopolis while working as an editor on the local English language newspaper by night. Phillip drove a magnificent red MG on his days off but was always short of money. Just before Christmas, the three of us took the overnight train to Luxor and were almost consumed by the sand blowing in through the windows of our overcrowded carriage. We stayed in a very basic pension on the same side of the river as the Valley of the Kings because Irene wished to write about the nearby village of New Gourna, built by Hassan Fathy, an important contemporary architect whose aim was to create functional modern villages along traditional lines. To explore the tombs of the kings, Phillip and I were offered donkeys as the only form of transport available – adequate but not comfortable. Thus, on Christmas Day we found ourselves sitting alone in the brilliant sunshine consuming the leftovers from our dinner the night before – tough camel, we reckoned. There was not a tourist within a hundred miles and apparently not even a custodian with a key to the tombs!

Luckily, such a person suddenly turned up, as if he had risen out of the very desert itself. All the tombs were opened one by one: the frescoes were breathtaking and still complete, their colours intense. Only now do I realise how extraordinarily lucky we were. The custodian left us to explore. He went back out into the sun, crouched in the sand and waited until we had gazed our fill.

Phillip and I then made an expedition further up the Nile in the new and unbearably noisy hydrofoil, without Irene, who wanted to remain near New Gourna to continue with her research. That winter of 1962/63 presented our only opportunity to see the Temple of Abu Simbel, built in honour of the deified Pharaoh Ramesses II, in its original position on the west bank of the Nile, before it was moved to avoid being flooded by the new Aswan Dam. The sun's rays were just striking the depths of the interior as we disembarked at noon. The façade, decorated with four colossal figures of Ramesses hewn out of the rock, towered over us. It was worth the six-hour round trip. Also fascinating to see were the colourful Nubian villages strung along the riverbanks; all soon to be submerged after the completion of the Aswan Dam. The clay houses were decorated with bright orange paint and their owners, with their much darker skin, were tall, thin, good-looking people. We were almost in Sudan.

We had arranged to rejoin Irene in a modern town near Abydos, where the government had just opened a sugar beet factory. Little did we think that Irene would be meeting our train, at one o'clock in the morning, under heavy police escort. We all spent the remainder of the night in a distinctly primitive hotel with police sitting in the corridor outside our bedroom doors. I slept in my clothes and cotton sun hat to avoid contact with the bedding. Without breakfast, we were marched off to the local courtroom and wasted much time watching the Chief of Police being shaved while he sipped his coffee. Irene was accused of intending to spread subversive propaganda. She had been caught photographing the *fellahin* (villagers) eating their lunch of broad beans and flat bread at long trestle tables in the town square. Although the town had a new factory to provide proper employment, the local scene did not reflect Nasser's boasts of immediate prosperity. This situation was central to Irene's forthcoming book on the social conditions of modern Egypt. Finally, armed with her press card, she argued her way to safety.

Transport was arranged for us to cross the Nile to the ruins of the Temple of Seti I in Abydos, where we were to meet its eccentric English keeper, Dorothy Eady, with her flying mane of grey hair, known locally as 'Om Seti' ('Mother of Seti'). She had lived there for many years and was famous for believing that she had been a priestess in ancient Egypt in a previous life. She waved what looked like a lavatory brush, and young men leapt into action and brought us lunch of hot hard-boiled eggs, warm flat bread and thick soup. We fell on the food: we had not eaten for twenty-four hours.

That night, Irene took us to stay at a small Jesuit monastery where she argued endlessly with the monks about how immoral it was to allow the Muslim population of this fly-ridden village to squat in the dust and filth while those who had converted to Christianity were provided with clean huts and weaving skills conducive to gainful employment. We spent New Year's Eve with these unsympathetic types and sipped some very treacly liquor to celebrate the occasion. It was all very sombre.

Upper Egypt had been an outstanding experience, but it was not the last. In the spring, I went off to the Oasis of Siwa with Salman and Frank. We drove my Renault Dauphine along the North African coast towards the Libyan border. At Mersa Matruh, where Cleopatra's fleet had once been based, also the site of a famous battle during the Western Desert campaign in 1940, we turned south into the desert and followed a line of old telegraph poles which stretched as far as the eye could see. We were retracing the footsteps of Alexander the Great, who had made a historic trip to Siwa to hear the oracle of Ammon. On the way, we were caught in a very frightening sandstorm, with lashing rain. When it had passed, we had to dig the car out of the sand and Salman sucked and spat the grit out of the clogged carburettor, as he had learned to do in his childhood in the Himalayas. Luckily, we managed to finish the journey in a burst of sunshine, and green plants bloomed in the wet sand as we watched.

Our reception at the Oasis was cordial. We were offered the one large bedroom to share in the guesthouse and were entertained for dinner by the Chief of Police. Early on in the evening, it dawned on me that he thought he was entertaining three young men, so short was my hair and so loose were my shirt and trousers. The women in the village also mistook us for three young men: they shied away from me and wrapped their thick, coloured cotton veils (like tablecloths) even more firmly round their heads and faces. I only saw their black eyes peering at me through dark folds. However, none of this proved a problem until after lunch the next day, when we were invited to take coffee and smoke the hookah with the elders of the village. Sitting on the floor in a circle in an upper room of this large house, the pipe came nearer and nearer, and my heart sank. All eyes were on me, and I could see not only expectation but also the first signs of alarm mirrored in their faces. Suddenly, one of the younger fellows rose to his feet, pointing at me fiercely and indicating the door and the floor below. The game was up! I was firmly marched downstairs to the mud basement where the women were cooing over their babies in the dark. I felt acutely embarrassed, and even more so when they started trying to communicate with me in Arabic and with hand signals – pointing at my ring finger and miming rocking a baby – about my marital prospects.

This trip was amongst the last of my adventures in Egypt. On the way back to Cairo, we stopped long enough at Mersa Matruh, close to the Libyan border, to visit the marketplace. We were not made to feel very welcome and did not stay long. It was chilling to think that nearby was Rommel's hideout during the Western Desert campaign. We also paused at El Alamein to see the war graves, which were very moving.

Back in my flat in Cairo, Salah, my *sufraghi* – old enough to be my grandfather – was anxiously awaiting my return. These trips worried him. Each morning, he would appear before seven o'clock to make my breakfast and escort me downstairs to my car carrying my English-language newspaper. While I was at the embassy, he went to the market, washed and ironed my clothes, and prepared my lunch. I never lifted a finger. At night, I simply stepped out of my clothes and fell into bed. When I was ill, he stayed all day and looked after me. My flat was in Zamalek, on the beautiful Gezira Island in the middle of the Nile. While lying in bed, I could see the pyramids in the distance, and while lying on the back of my sofa in the sitting room, I could watch the *feluccas* sailing by. I wept when I returned to this place again in 1987. It had become a rowdy concrete jungle, full of American-style hotels and thick with modern traffic. The drive through the villages of the verdant Delta to the pyramids had been swallowed up by this urban scene, as had the weaving school set up by the Egyptian architect, Wissa Wassef, that we had visited so often with Frank.

I left Cairo with many regrets in late August 1963. I had been tempted to stay on, but I realised that without the embassy umbrella it would have been foolish. I had made so many interesting friends in both the Egyptian community and amongst contemporaries in several embassies. I had had the privilege of working for the press secretary, Michael Weir (many years later the British Ambassador to Egypt), who was always buried in the Arab newspapers when I arrived in his office. I feel I should have understood the political situation more clearly but, of course, as secretaries, we were not encouraged to get involved in political questions. I also rode in the desert with the Head of Chancery, Sir Donald Hawley, who always talked about his posting in Abu Dhabi (then still part of the Trucial States in the eastern Persian Gulf). However, perhaps my greatest friend was Mursi Saad El Din, a journalist and a great favourite with everyone at the embassy. I think he was relied upon for introductions to, and information about, the Egyptian intelligentsia and government officials in Cairo. On Fridays, he used to invite the three English secretaries to lunch on grilled prawns at his literary club and tell us about his trips to the PEN Club in London. He gave me books written by local authors and tried to open my eyes to a more sophisticated Egyptian milieu. I never fully appreciated his efforts, which I regret.

When I embarked with my car at Alexandria for my return to London, to my horror, the customs authorities ripped off the Arabic licence plates because I no longer had diplomatic immunity. This definitively underlined my departure from this magical land. Reality struck once more when I tried to land in Brindisi two days later. There was a huge drama at the customs house about there being no plates on this foreign car but, finally, an Italian compromise was reached, and handwritten cardboard plates were provided for the journey to Rome. Once in Rome, the British Embassy obliged by providing smart metal plates, which got me back to London without further ado. However, because my car had been registered in Egypt but had not been eligible for diplomatic plates, the numbers were still in Arabic script and the plates still labelled 'Cairo'. My Uncle Robert did not want the car parked in front of their house in Chelsea. He had served as an officer in the British army in Egypt after the Second World War, and was not keen on being identified with what he called 'those very tricky people'. At considerable expense, I had to re-register the car in England, as it had initially been registered in Belgium, where I had learnt to drive in it.

======

CHAPTER 13

In Florence

My next plan, formulated with my friends in Cairo and particularly Phillip Ward Green, was to apply for a place at The Courtauld Institute of Art in London. The ambassador in Cairo, Sir Harold Beeley, for whom I sometimes typed dispatches, wrote to his friend from Cambridge days, the director of The Courtauld, Anthony Blunt, and asked him to give me an interview. Instead, I was interviewed by his colleague Dr Margaret Whinney, who enthusiastically suggested a year in Florence, as places for the forthcoming year (1963/64) were already filled. This seemed like an exciting challenge, so I climbed back into my car and set off, with the blessing of Aunt Lulu and Uncle Robert, with whom I had been staying. My plan was to study Italian and absorb as much as possible of the Early Renaissance before reapplying to The Courtauld in the spring.

With the help of my cousin Richard Fremantle, who lived in a medieval tower in central Florence, I found a flat on the rooftops opposite the Loggia dei Lanzi in Piazza della Signoria. It was a delightfully bohemian setup with a view of Cellini's *Perseus* from the sitting room. There were a bedroom and study under the eaves, a wood stove I was afraid to light, and no hot water. I survived it for the best part of a year and worked in front of a large electric fire to keep out the chill. I had my Canadian friends the Morgensterns to stay and even dared to invite the distinguished scholar, writer and aesthete, Harold Acton, and Ian Greenlees, director of the British Institute, for drinks. Acton and Greenlees were bosom companions, and very kind to me in Florence. I was invited to their dinner parties, where the conversation always turned, with ruthless humour, to those absent – very amusing but also rather alarming! I learnt Italian at the British Institute and, in exchange, taught an English evening class to Italian Air Force pilots. They were charming and handsome but not very quick to learn. To fund my travels in Italy, I also taught Shakespeare at a fashionable girls' school at the Medici Villa of Poggio Imperiale, above the Porta Romana, and English to eight-year-olds at a convent school. Here, the nuns kept the class in order, so I only had to concentrate on getting the language across. I enjoyed both these jobs but felt so sorry for the homesick boarders at Poggio Imperiale. They would beg me to post secret letters to their boyfriends.

The highlight of that year was a ten-day trip round Sicily over Easter with two friends from the Villa I Tatti – Ron Witt and Price Zimmermann, both working on their doctoral theses on Renaissance history. I Tatti was the villa previously owned by the art connoisseur and scholar Bernard Berenson, which now served as the Harvard University Center for Italian Renaissance Studies. We followed in the footsteps of Berenson's last tour of the island, an account of which he had published in 1955. However, on Good Friday we diverged from it at a place called Sciacca, for lack of accommodation anywhere else. We had to settle for a soulless ACI motel in the middle of this dreary town, but, most fortunately, there was a reward. We followed a crowd to the main square, under heavy grey skies, and there we saw a spectacular and very moving Holy Week procession re-enacting not only Christ's ascent to Calvary, but also the actual nailing of his body (a plaster effigy) to the cross, all done in Late Medieval costume and with immense ceremony. I wept!

I made more good friends at I Tatti through Ron and Price. The director was the distinguished Italian history professor, Myron Gilmour. A large and very kind American lady called Esther Sperry, who lived in one of the properties about the main villa, used to arrange day-outings by car to see the village churches that Berenson had rediscovered. We were taken to see the now much-acclaimed Pontormo, *Visitation*, hanging over the high altar in the church at Carmignano for which it was commissioned. We had to find the sacristan for the key and then peer through the gloom of the unlit church to see the painting's remarkable composition and intense colour.

My year in Tuscany had been much enhanced by the presence of Richard Fremantle, whose grandmother, Tiny Grant Duff, was my great-aunt. He was very gregarious and gave fantastic parties in his tower almost every weekend. I loved him and made many friends through him. Richard was famous for his many lady friends, though his later marriage to the artist Chloë Eley lasted eleven years. We kept in close touch until his death in 2019.

CHAPTER 14

Student Days at The Courtauld Institute

Although heavily frowned on by Uncle Peter, my two years at The Courtauld Institute working for the Post-Graduate Diploma were even more rewarding than I had expected. Uncle Peter had promised my mother he would find me 'a handsome husband with ten thousand a year' but, so far, he had not succeeded; I realised years later that the relations had hoped I might hang on in the Foreign Service and marry a dashing diplomat. He took me out to lunch and said that if I wanted to go to The Courtauld, I would have to fund myself. This was not a deterrent, as I had put aside sufficient funds already: due to Foreign Office policy, only one-third of my salary in Egypt was paid in Egyptian pounds; the rest was paid directly into my English bank account, which I could not access from abroad. Thus, I had effectively saved a large part of my salary. The student's steady diet of spam and tinned salmon was grim, but I relied heavily on invitations out to dinner and, luckily, got them.

One ray of hope for the family was my intense friendship with a brilliant and highly intellectual French lawyer working at the Conseil d'État in Paris. I met the charming Roger Herrera through a friend in Florence in the summer of 1965, and our relationship lasted about a year. He used to send me the weekly copy of *Le Monde* to improve my French and gave me beautiful art books, which I still have. He introduced me to the films of Alain Resnais and Luis Buñuel and took me with him to hear François Mitterand speak at the Assemblée Nationale. Aunt Paddy was horrified and said Roger must be a communist. I was shocked: such an idea had never crossed my mind! We went to Morocco for a week at the New Year. Roger had a friend in Marrakech who invited us to dinner in a large and picturesque, typically Moroccan house with a grapefruit tree growing in the walled garden. These were the days before mass tourism, so the famous Jemaa el-Fnaa Square was totally unspoilt – even the tame monkey and the bear seemed to be a genuine part of the local scene. We drove through the spectacular Atlas Mountains, which reminded me of the mountains in Leonardo da Vinci's drawings. We also went to Fez, which felt like stepping back into the Middle Ages with its stone walls and narrow, winding streets. However, we could have done without the tour of the tannery there: the smell was unbearable.

Sadly, our relationship floundered just before my final exams at The Courtauld in May 1966. I was shattered but somehow managed to get through them, with the unexpected and sympathetic support of my tutors John Shearman and Michael Kitson. Roger was from a very intellectual Jewish background, and I was not confident enough to rise to the challenge that presented. I think he was afraid to marry outside his own orbit, and I made the mistake of not introducing him to Uncle Peter and Aunt Paddy, who wanted to meet him, so he never understood my background. Aunt Lulu comforted me with the words, 'It is safer to marry your own race', advice which would not be appropriate today.

Our paths crossed again in Rome about four years later, a city we had explored together and that, by this time, my husband John and I had made our home. I met Roger with his wife while walking near the Pantheon one March day. Roger and I were very pleased to see each other, and I invited him and his wife to dinner at our flat in the Via Dandolo, on the Janiculum Hill. We had John's best man, Donald Moyer, staying with us, and our baby daughter Emily was ill, but we managed to pull together a feast. John and Donald were both deeply intrigued and had been primed to make intellectual conversation – luckily, it could be in English, as Roger arrived without his wife, who claimed a headache. We had a very convivial evening, and I sensed that, for both of us, it was a lovely trip down memory lane. Except for a meeting over coffee two days later in a bar in Piazza del Popolo with Roger's wife, also a lawyer and rather distant, I have never seen him again. Curiously, John's sister Jenny knew one of his friends when she and her husband David were living in Paris. She offered to arrange a meeting, but I declined. I often wonder if that was a mistake. It would have been almost twenty years later.

My years at The Courtauld coincided with a golden age. I was taught by Andrew Martindale, John Shearman, Anthony Blunt and both Michael Hirst and Michael Kitson. The Institute was still in Home House, the Adam house in Portman Square bought by Samuel Courtauld. However, over-stuffed tall metal bookcases obscured much of the fine Adam decoration. Anthony Blunt's office was off the elegant marble bathroom where his secretary sat. At Portman Square, the Institute was much smaller than it is today at Somerset House, and relatively relaxed. We were more like a large group of friends, all in pursuit of art history. On sunny days, the Common Room tea party moved out into the garden. I remember sitting on a bench with Julian Gardner (a well-known Late Medieval scholar) while he kindly explained how to read plans and elevations for fifteenth-century gothic churches. Meanwhile, Timothy Clifford, the gregarious future director of the National Galleries of Scotland, would be holding court in the opposite corner.

Unbeknownst to us at this time, Professor Blunt was secretly making his full confession about his espionage activities to the Security Services. He was, on the whole, popular with his students and certainly with the staff, and a most enthusiastic teacher. His lectures, in which he strode rapidly back and forth across the stage with his gown flying out behind him, were always well attended. During a tutorial in his study on Nicolas Poussin's drawings, I remember him sprinting up the library ladder to retrieve an original edition of published letters between Poussin and his important French patron, Paul Fréart de Chantelou.

John Shearman's was not an easy personality but he was an inspiring teacher. I was fortunate to have had him for all my tutorials on the early Italian Renaissance, and I learnt more from his analytical approach than from anyone else in my entire academic life. He insisted his students go frequently to the National Gallery and spend half an hour in front of each relevant painting; we were to return with a complete understanding of style and content. This habit has stayed with me always. Shearman did not allow us to use social history to explain the art or the artist – as is the practice in art history today. We were trained to rely on connoisseurship and documentary evidence. As a special treat, he arranged to take us to see Count Seilern's collection in his drawing room at Prince's Gate. I spent days preparing an essay on Piero della Francesca, whose precise geometric style and intellectual approach fascinated me. The obscure meaning of some of his paintings had been analysed by American scholars who were already addressing social art history, and I drew on their ideas with relish. After listening to the essay, John sniffed audibly. 'Do you believe all you read?' he asked, scathingly. I was crushed.

Years later, John Shearman contacted me in Rome while researching in the Hertziana Library in his holidays. I think he was lonely and on a British academic's budget, so he wolfed down the steak I offered him for dinner – his lunch would have been a pocket coffee in a bar! I offered to drive him to an isolated fifteenth-century church near Aquila one Saturday if he could keep our children Emily and Jocelyn entertained in the back seat of the car, whilst

John did the difficult map-reading. To our amazement, he was brilliant with them, even reading them Asterix books.

Michael Kitson, beloved of all students, could be found surrounded by them at lunchtime in the local pub. Michael taught me to appreciate seventeenth-century landscape paintings, most especially those of Claude and Rembrandt. I met my life-long friend, Nicky Coldstream, in Michael's tutorial group. She was to become a distinguished medieval architectural historian. Ernst Gombrich and Nikolaus Pevsner used to come up from the Warburg Institute to give us lectures. I realised that this was a great privilege, but I found their Germanic English accents too guttural for my ear and my concentration would falter – my loss! Jennifer Montagu also came, to talk about small bronzes, and I remember thinking her very glamorous.

I had just enough money set aside to pay the tuition fees and for lodgings round the corner. I rented a room in a cottage in Gloucester Mews from a very hearty but (I thought) quite mad antique furniture dealer called Elizabeth. Elizabeth knew everyone in London and gave me a lot of good advice, and several good dinners, when she was in town. I never knew when I came home in the evenings whether I would find the same furniture in place – at least she never sold the bed I slept in!

During this period of my life, my mother, still in Canada, decided I was perhaps scholarly enough to meet her old friends the Wingfield Digbys, with whom we had stayed during the first winter of the war. Although George's passion was for modern British pottery and oriental porcelain, he had become Keeper of Textiles at the Victoria and Albert Museum and ran the department with great skill. I stayed with George and Nellie for about six weeks between flats and got to know them very well. George was writing a book on twentieth-century British pottery, so they invited me to go with them to St Ives to meet Bernard Leach. They also introduced me to Krishnamurti, a famous follower of Ouspensky. He lectured on topics such as anxiety, pointing out that worry was a great time-waster. George never spoke at dinner after these evening lectures; for him, they were like an intense religious experience.

CHAPTER 15

V&A

In the late summer of 1967, my Courtauld qualification led to a job at the Victoria and Albert Museum as a research assistant in the now-defunct Circulation Department. George Wingfield Digby kindly stood as a character reference and Michael Kitson as an academic one. Again, Uncle Peter took me out to lunch and said, 'Out of the frying pan into the fire. Joining the V&A will be like entering a nunnery!' It only fully occurred to me then that the family saw marriage as far more important than my career in art history. I was letting the family down: I must marry!

The eccentric Circulation Department was responsible for touring exhibitions, curated from the V&A's large reserve collections, around the major provincial museums of the British Isles. I was one of five research assistants, each in charge of a section of the country. One selected one's own theme and did the research, design and layout for each exhibition. In a large storeroom off our gallery were huge bolts of material in a variety of rich colours. From these, one chose a decorative ground for the display, hoping to minimise the heaviness of the old-fashioned showcases. I chose Coptic textiles for my first exhibition, in memory of my time in Egypt, followed by medieval pots (rather surprisingly), and then theatre costume design – which brought me closer to the prints and drawings not on offer in my department. In many ways, I was a square peg in a round hole, as the major interests of the other curators were nineteenth-century objects – glass, silver, porcelain – and they concentrated on these for both their exhibitions and further research. Eventually, I applied for transfer to the Prints and Drawings Department, under the directorship of John Pope-Hennessey.

My first weeks at the museum were not easy. The men in the department saw me as an ex-Courtauld 'debutante'. Anthony Radcliffe, also a research assistant, and later distinguished for his work on small Italian bronzes, rounded on me fiercely from the doorway of his neighbouring office: 'What right have you to accept a job as a woman, on a salary equal to mine? You have not got a family to feed and no obvious need for money! Of course, you went to The Courtauld Institute and I only read history at Cambridge!'

As Uncle Peter had pointed out, in England in the late Sixties it was perceived that only 'bluestockings' worked in museums or academic circles. At the auction houses, women could apply as secretaries but no more, and the art world was still a man's world. I had been warned by Nellie Wingfield Digby not to go to the hairdresser before my interview at the V&A and not to wear smart clothes. Fortunately, Anthony Radcliffe learned to feel less threatened and became both friendly and helpful. I remember being very flattered when Ronald Lightbown, Keeper of Metalwork, invited me to his house for dinner. Like my mother at Mulberry Walk, I feared having nothing to say. Academics had their own language.

I met John's sister, Jenny, while working in Circulation. She was a museum assistant and chosen to work with me as she, too, was perceived to be part of the 'privileged class' of women who did not belong. Over the dreary trial of sorting out the department's metalwork collection (mainly locks and keys), we quickly became firm friends. She introduced me to her brother, John, whom she had decided I should marry. Ironically, when, in due course, I decided I would marry John and leave the V&A to live with him in Rome, trouble came again, this time from the eminent lady scholars in Circulation. They decided to boycott me – not for getting married but for resigning. I had spoilt their case for hiring more women: I had proved how fickle women employees were. Happily, Barbara Morris, well known for her work on Victorian glass, remained a supporter, and she generously helped design my wedding dress using the museum's collection of Regency pattern books.

Initially, we all worked under the museum's director, Trenchard Cox, who was warm and encouraging to all, including the families of the warders. When he retired, he was replaced by the eminent scholar of Italian Renaissance sculpture, John Pope-Hennessey, whose powerful voice echoing down the long corridors was reminiscent of that of the Cumaean Sybil rumbling in her lair. In those days, there were not thousands of museum visitors, so the staff could wander through the collections at leisure. We all carried long thin pass keys which opened all the heavy showcases. We thought of the collections as being our own and visitors as occasional intruders. Curators, then called keepers, understood the job to be an opportunity to concentrate on their own research and wrote their books in office hours. We were permitted to take vast quantities of books out of the library at one time and hide away in our offices to read them. It was another world.

CHAPTER 16

The Ormonds

Our wedding, accompanied by glorious music, took place on 20 April 1968 in the Church of Our Most Holy Redeemer and Saint Thomas More, Chelsea. Uncle Peter said of the music that it was like experiencing a particularly beautiful concert at the Festival Hall. He had achieved his goal at last and happily agreed to give me away. My mother and stepbrother David came from Canada and all the Agnew aunts and Uncle Colin turned out to support her.

John and Flavia on their wedding day, 20 April 1968

I felt at home with John's family, as our lives had in many ways already been travelling along parallel lines. John and I had met as a result of the prejudiced treatment Jenny and I had received at the V&A, which had forged such a close friendship between us, but there were many other connections. John's parents had rented Fig Tree Court from my great-aunt Edith Grant Duff in the late Thirties, and thus had met my favourite aunt, Lulu Boyle. John's father had sat behind my father's first cousin, Conradine Hobhouse, at a Chelsea primary school and had dipped her pigtails in the inkwell. At the beginning of the Second World War, the Ormond family, as refugees from London, had stayed with the Hobhouses at Hadspen, their eighteenth-century house in Somerset; John had shared the school-room with Hermione Hobhouse, later to become an expert on Victorian architecture. John had been invited to Lerici near the Cinque Terre to read to the writer Percy Lubbock, my grandmother's first cousin. We were, apparently, the first two children to be photographed by a famous Thirties society photographer. And so on. However, I had never heard of John's great-uncle, John Singer Sargent, the famous American portrait painter (1856–1925) as I had never looked at art post-1750. Now, years later, I cannot imagine having had such a narrow approach. Uncle Peter was, of course, delighted by this connection, and my mother urged me to go quickly to the Tate (Britain), where some of Sargent's finest works were to be seen. John's parents' house was, in fact, liberally hung with Sargent's splendid pictures, which they appeared to accept as perfectly natural. Indeed, Sargent was a prolific artist and, when he died, his sisters Emily and Violet, overwhelmed by the amount of work left in his studio, generously gave paintings, drawings and watercolours to a number of prominent museums. The rest were distributed to members of the family.

Aunt Lulu was fascinated by our engagement, as she remembered Dorothea, John's beautiful mother, from the Fig Tree Court days. When I rang one evening to say John was in London and could I bring him round, her response was, 'Yes, but give us fifteen minutes to finish dinner.' When we duly arrived, Aunt Lulu and Uncle Robert were sitting in the drawing room in full evening dress with a bottle of white wine freshly opened and four glasses. John was deeply impressed and had no idea that they had swallowed their scrambled-egg supper and created a Thirties-style reception in that short space of time. Thus, when we went to stay with them at their country house in Sussex, John packed both his dinner jacket and a smart tweed suit. I think he was most relieved to find it was a 'wellies' weekend without parties.

Family anecdotes allowed me to piece together a broader picture of the Sargent/Ormond family and their pursuit of an intellectual life enriched by music, art and travel. John's father, Conrad, used to regale his children with stories of meeting the novelist Henry James at tea with Conrad's mother, Sargent's youngest sister Violet. He observed that Henry James conversed as he wrote – in a slow, ponderous manner. One day at tea, an American friend turned to James and said, 'May I fix you a cup of tea?'

My dear young lady', he replied, 'you interest me exceedingly. What will you fix it with and what will you fix it to?'

John was very fond of his grandmother Violet and spent a lot of time with her on days out from Westminster School, where he was a boarder. Violet was living in Carlyle Mansions in Cheyne Walk, Chelsea, and John would find himself sharing the lift with personalities such as T.S. Eliot and Eliot's editor and archivist, John Hayward, who also lived there. John and Violet went to concerts together, but always by bus, as Violet thought taxis an extravagance even in her old age.

Violet and her Swiss husband, Francis Ormond, actually met in San Remo where his mother had a house, known today as the Villa Ormond. The Sargents, who were in San Remo staying with a friend, did not approve of this often charming but peppery little man. However, Violet was determined to have him! All his life, Francis was in the habit of running away to seek adventure. Before his marriage, he ran off to Canada and, apparently, worked on the construction of the Canadian National Railway. After their wedding, he and Violet travelled widely, and, consequently, all the children were born abroad – Marguerite in Barcelona; Rose Marie in Tunis; Jean-Louis, Guillaume and Conrad (John's father) in the Ormond grandmother's house at San Remo; and Reine in Paris. After long sojourns in Majorca and Barcelona, and the arrival of six children, the Ormonds finally chose to settle down in London, near John Singer Sargent and his older sister Emily in Chelsea. However, Francis was still restless, and another house was bought in Tunis before he disappeared on his own to seek another adventure in the South Seas – especially Tahiti, where he apparently acquired, among other things, a Gauguin portrait.[1]

The three younger children of Francis and Violet lived with their mother in England, but the three eldest were brought up in San Remo and Switzerland on the insistence of the ever-powerful Ormond grandmother. Francis had refused to follow in his father's footsteps and run the family tobacco firm in Vevey, but his eldest son, Jean-Louis, was to be given no choice. The six brothers

John and Flavia on the cliffs near Truro,
Cornwall, March 1968

and sisters were only reunited for summer walking holidays in the Alps, organised by their father, Francis. In old age, Jean-Louis expressed much bitterness at having been taken away from his mother as a child.

Violet was always part of artistic London circles. After the First World War, she had given financial help to the dancer Vaslav Nijinsky so that he could marry. He had been left penniless because the founder of the Ballets Russes, Sergei Diaghilev, deeply wounded by what he considered this betrayal, had demanded that Nijinsky leave the company. Violet took Francis to hear Salvador Dali give his lecture on Surrealism in 1936. Dali foolishly wore a genuine diving suit for the occasion. When he started struggling for breath, because the suit would not come off as planned, Francis laughed so raucously that Violet had to remove him from the scene.

Guillaume, the eldest of the English set of children, always spoke English with a Swiss-French accent. He read music at Oxford and became the organist and Master of the Choristers at Truro Cathedral for the next forty years. He was the much-loved eccentric member of the family and very generous to his nieces and nephews. Once, when we were staying with him, he bought a whole afternoon tea, complete with cups and saucers, from a shop in Truro to take with us so that we could all enjoy the late afternoon sun on a beautiful cliff walk.

A famous family story of Guillaume's delightful vagueness describes him knocking on a cottage door in Truro because he could hear one of his favourite pieces of Bach being played. The owners invited him in but said they could not offer him tea as they were about to leave for an organ concert at the cathedral. 'Oh', said Guillaume, looking at his watch. 'I am giving it', and he rushed from the room. John was very fond of this uncle and, in many ways, like him, sharing his love and talent for music. John was amused by Guillaume's passion for smart cars, motorboats and photography, although he did not share in those passions himself.

Guillaume and his elder brother Jean-Louis always spent their holidays together, looking at pictures in various European museums. Jean-Louis's house in Vevey was earthquake-proof and filled with heavy German renaissance furniture. There was a fine collection of German carved statuettes and several Sargents on the walls. Like Guillaume, Jean-Louis never married. He was a keen and highly respected chess player, playing in tournaments and by correspondence even into old age. He was very handsome but also shy, and it took me a long time to realise how genuinely fond he was of his family. He hated anyone being unpunctual, so when John and I first stayed with him, and he saw I was not wearing a watch, he immediately bought me one.

Jean-Louis's two eldest sisters, with whom he grew up in San Remo and Switzerland, had sad lives. The eldest, Marguerite, had serious mental health problems, and spent much of her life in a sanatorium. The younger sister, Rose-Marie, died in Paris on Good Friday 1918, when a German shell struck the Church of St Gervais where she was attending a concert. Her husband, Robert André-Michel, a French art historian, had been killed in action in October 1914 on the Aisne, only an hour's drive from, and one month after, the battle that claimed the life of my grandfather, Adrian Grant Duff. Rose-Marie had been Sargent's favourite model and had posed for many watercolours on their family summer holidays in the Val d'Aosta. She loved music, like so many members of the family, and concerts became her solace as a widow in war-torn Paris.

Violet's youngest daughter Reine and her devoted husband, Hugo Pitman, bought Dante Gabriel Rossetti's Tudor House, at 16 Cheyne Walk, next door to Violet and Francis. They also acquired the seventeenth-century Manor House at Odstock, a village near Salisbury, where they entertained their creative and intellectual friends – among whom were Cecil Beaton and Truman Capote. Their younger daughter Jemima, who loved Odstock, related to me that her parents enjoyed buying contemporary pictures from both Augustus and Gwen John, who lived nearby, and the Glasgow painter Ethel Walker, amongst others.

Both Reine and Conrad studied at the Slade School of Art. Conrad, learning to model in sculpture, asked John's mother, Dorothea (not yet his wife), to pose full length. Sadly, the resulting terracotta nude later disappeared, thought to have been smashed by Conrad because he didn't feel it did her justice.[2]

(l-r) Jenny, Tim, John and Richard Ormond at Emily Ormond's wedding,
Sheppard's Farm, June 2006

Conrad had met Dorothea Gibbons as a bachelor guest of his friend Jock
Cumberledge, who was married to one of her sisters. They were introduced
at a house party held at Stanwell Place, Middlesex, the Gibbons family home
which the 2nd Baronet Sir John Gibbons (1717–1776) had acquired in 1760
after returning from Barbados, where his father had been Lieutenant-General.[3]
At the time, Dorothea was married to her first husband Ernest Byng, a man
20 years older than she, and they were living in Warwickshire with their two
small children, Robert and Jane. However, when she met Conrad Ormond,
it was love at first sight and there was no going back, she told me many years
later. She and Conrad were married quietly in 1934. John and Tim, born
close together in 1934 and 1935, always felt under-loved. Their parents were
probably not ready for children at this point in their relationship, and both
John and Tim were sent to boarding school at the age of seven. John's only
happy memories of childhood seem to have been Christmas Day and summer
holidays on beaches in Cornwall. When his youngest brother Richard was
born, and four years later his sister Jenny, John felt thoroughly pushed out of
his mother's affections. He used to recount the time he pushed Richard into a
dustbin and sat on the lid with a mixture of glee and guilt.

Conrad and his brothers placed a great deal of importance on staying in touch with each other and with Switzerland. After the war, in 1947, Conrad and Dorothea took their three sons to stay with Jean-Louis. They spent a month at his seventeenth-century farmhouse overlooking Vevey and Lake Geneva. Cécile, Jean-Louis' young housekeeper, loved to recall this visit: three wild boys, John, Tim and Richard, rampaging around this bachelor establishment. Richard remembered that on the journey home, somewhere in France, their car had a serious puncture. Due to currency regulations, they had no money; in any case, there were no tyres to buy! However, the Frenchman to whom they turned for help gave them one of his tyres, as he recalled how supportive of the French the British were during the war.

1: With thanks to June Hargrove and Richard Ormond for this information.

2: *A Woven Life*, Jenny Housego; The Lotus Collection, An imprint of Roli Books Ltd, 2020, p. 15–16.

3: The first Baronet Sir William Gibbons, born in Britain, became Speaker of the Assembly and Lieutenant-General of Barbados, and owned many of the notorious sugar plantations worked by slaves. His son, the second Baronet, became a British Member of Parliament. The large Stanwell estate was sold in the 1930s, and the property is now incorporated into Heathrow Airport.

CHAPTER 17

The Great Escape

John, aptly named after his great-uncle John Singer Sargent, was, like his Uncle Guillaume, refreshingly eccentric, and looked at life through Edwardian spectacles. He was a romantic who shied away from the conventions of modern life and its emphasis on achievement for its own sake. After all my years in chauvinistic Canada, I found these qualities delightful! Usually referred to as John Francis by his mother's family to distinguish him from his mother's brother, Sir John Gibbons, he had inherited his mother's handsome looks. He was perceived as an introspective person, like his father, but he also shared his father's charm and generosity. However, I never thought of John as quiet. He used to talk to me for hours on end and patiently filled in great gaps in my knowledge of history and music. He was a great reader, especially of history and biography, and blessed with a phenomenal memory. He had read history at Christ Church but, sadly, did not enjoy Oxford life. He used to reminisce about walking through the freezing cold cloister in order to have a bath. He inherited Sargent's love of music and a fine singing voice. On the rare occasions we went to church, other people would turn round to listen to him. Not being in the least vain, he was totally unaware of the effect he was having! Years later, he entertained our children with rousing renditions of the Neapolitan folk song, *Santa Lucia*. Our life together was made up of complete companionship – we loved the same things, and travelling was our passion.

Our married life began with a two-month honeymoon rambling round Turkey. I found the mosques in Istanbul very interesting, but the atmosphere of the city was not nearly as exotic as Cairo's, and I was disappointed. It was relatively run-down in 1968, and there were stray cats everywhere. However, our trip down the west coast of Anatolia by local bus was an extraordinary adventure. Our fellow travellers in the buses were often accompanied by their goats and chickens. There were no hotels or B&Bs along the way, so we stayed in simple local cottages with huge stork nests on the roofs. Travelling this way, we visited completely deserted Greco-Roman sites: no ticket wickets, and no tourists. Troy had been high on our list, but the day we went there was particularly hot and it was difficult to comprehend the various layers of the excavations. We had expected to find more expansive ruins to evoke the famous site of the Trojan War. Ephesus was far more exciting. Although the extensive complex was completely unrestored, we were able to clamber all over the ruins trying to make sense of the spaces and, most particularly for John, of the famous library. We followed an old guidebook. Often, we had to negotiate with local taxis to get to sites off the beaten track. This was true near Antalya, where we wished to see the huge necropolis at Termessos, high above sea level in beautiful mountains. The road was full of potholes, and the driver had never previously been asked to go there. He was not keen. However, the carved stone tombs, many with their lids pushed off, were a rewarding sight. Made for the famous local warriors, they were overgrown with a tangle of wild vegetation which attracted masses of butterflies. I have never forgotten this scene, so reminiscent of engravings by Giovanni Battista Piranesi, the eighteenth-century Italian printmaker famous for his bizarre pastiches of antique Roman buildings. Likewise, the well-preserved Roman theatre at Aspendos, with cows grazing in the adjoining field, made us think of the seventeenth-century French landscape painter Claude Lorrain.

We also visited Perge, where St Paul preached his first sermon, and the hill site of the famous Pergamon altar, now reconstructed in the Pergamon Museum in Berlin. We had considered going to Ankara and trying to get involved in a dig at a Hittite site. John had studied for an archaeology diploma after taking his degree in modern history at Christ Church. However, the impracticality of this idea became evident, as we had no links with the archaeologists on the dig and nowhere to stay, so we stayed on the plane at Ankara and flew on to Cappadocia to see the Byzantine frescoes in the rock caves. We moved on to the Seljuk capital of Konya, where we saw Sufi dervishes whirling in front of one of the mosques, and then to Bursa, the first Ottoman capital, famous for its beautiful architecture. I do not remember whether John realised that Sargent had also been there, painting scenes of the mosques. I remember lots of red rose bushes and a luxuriously comfortable hotel.

John had dreamed of living in Rome, a city he had fallen in love with at least a year before he met and fell in love with me. Meeting me seemed to him to make his dream possible, and he persuaded me to share it. I weighed up in my mind what would be most exciting: staying on at the V&A, with the problems I had encountered there, or moving to this magical, beautiful city. I was young and adventurous and, being 'neither fish, nor fowl, nor good red herring', as my erstwhile antique-dealing landlady in London had once described me, the spirit of adventure prevailed.

Our plans for settling in Rome, a city we both knew well from previous travels, were now at hand. However, getting there took forty-eight hours from Istanbul, in four different trains with no couchettes, so we sat up all night. We nearly lost all our luggage at the station in Sofia, Bulgaria – it was simply taken off the train! Luckily, John saw it on the platform and rushed off the train to put it back on board. There was nothing to eat until we reached Venice, where, mercifully, we had time for a huge lunch before the next *Espresso* train to Rome. The restaurant was quite grand and expensive, and the waiters looked at us with curiosity, as we were both so ravenous and dishevelled.

We were instinctively following a path similar to that of the Sargent great-grandparents in the mid-nineteenth century: choosing a foreign country to live in because it seemed more beautiful and more fascinating than our own and we reckoned we had sufficient funds.[1] Our idea was an outmoded lifestyle by the late 1960s, but we looked back to people such as the American writer Iris Origo and the British writer Percy Lubbock, her step-father, as well as to John's grandparents Francis and Violet. There were still a number of foreign artists, musicians and writers living in Rome and seeking inspiration from the city's infinite charm. We were obliged to become 'British Residents Abroad' and to register our names with the Roman authorities for 'Permessi di Soggiorno', residency permits renewable on a yearly basis. We gave ourselves two years to create a niche; we managed to stay successfully for fifteen. We thought that we could bring our children up as citizens of Europe, and when Britain made its decision to join the Common Market in 1973 we felt very avant-garde. Writing in 2022, I am saddened to reflect on Britain's recent rejection of the European Union.

In the late Sixties Rome was still overwhelmingly romantic, with wildflowers growing out of every crevice in the ruins of the Forum and the Palatine. We could have undisturbed picnics in the Domus Flavia, and John would read aloud from Byron's *Childe Harold's Pilgrimage*. There were few cars, and, consequently, many small street markets for buying food. Wine was procured from a tap in the wall of the local wine shop. We spent the first summer just absorbing the beauty of the city and eating delicious *funghi porcini* and *tagliatelle al burro* in the local trattorias. I had never felt so hedonistic.

John introduced me to my own cousin, Jocelyn Lubbock, and his wife Georgette, who lived in a flat on a rooftop in the Via dei Pellegrini near Campo de' Fiori; Georgette was a passionate gardener, so the roof was smothered in flowers. John had made friends with them when reading to the writer Percy Lubbock, who was Jocelyn's uncle and Granny Grant Duff's first cousin, at Lerici in Liguria, in 1962–63.[2]

Jocelyn and Georgette gave us a very warm welcome on our arrival in Rome, and within a week had found us a small flat on the rooftop of a palazzo in the Via dei Coronari, near Piazza Navona, where we were woken every morning by the ringing of many church bells. Georgette was to become our daughter Emily's godmother.

Through their friendship with Professor John Ward-Perkins, the director of the British School at Rome, John was invited to research and sort out the archives there. He also spent some of his time there trying to write an article on the history of the Therebintus Neronis and the Meta Romuli, ancient Roman tombs traditionally associated with the site of the crucifixion of Saint Peter and depicted as such in Giotto's *Stefaneschi Triptych* (painted for Old St Peter's Basilica and now in the Vatican Museum). This was John's first attempt at writing for publication, but the manuscript is now lost. It was full of ideas about the location of these lost tombs and St Peter's crucifixion that were hard to prove.

In the late summer of 1968, a few months after we had started living in Rome, John's brother Richard and his wife Leonee came to visit us. On their first evening, Richard had his newly completed manuscript for a biography of Sargent stolen from the boot of their car while we were dining on our rooftop. In horror, they spent most of the night with John and the *carabinieri* searching in vain in every rubbish bin in the area. The suitcase contained all Leonee's clothes, and the manuscript was undoubtedly thrown away! Richard was amazingly controlled and subsequently dictated the whole book to Leonee, as best he remembered it, as they drove home across Italy and France.

In the autumn, we moved across the River Tiber to Trastevere and settled in the Via Roma Libera, overlooking the large daily market in the Piazza di San Cosimato. Still in Old Rome but in the old working-class quarter, the piazza was very lively. Many of the houses were without telephones, so the women called to each other from window to window all day long. Although relatively modern, our building did not possess a lift and most of the occupants still did their washing in a communal trough in the internal courtyard. The *portiera* was very large and very friendly. When Emily, newly born, came home from the hospital in February 1969, the *portiera* was waiting at the door to greet us. Five weeks later, in March 1969, the left-wing terrorist group soon to be formed into the *Brigate Rosse* (the Red Brigades) carried out one of its first bomb attacks, on the *Ministero dell' Istruzione Pubblica* (Ministry of Public Education) in the Viale Trastevere on the corner of our street. Many windows in our *palazzo* were shattered due to the force of the deafening diagonal blast. Our new friend's first thought was for the survival of the *bambina inglese*. Amid piercing screams from every doorway, she panted up four flights of stairs to see if all was well. Fortunately, Emily Violet slept peacefully through this life-threatening event, saved by the wooden shutters fastened against the damp night air. John and I, on the other hand, swept up alarming quantities of finely broken glass in our bedroom and front hall.

Emily Violet – named after Sargent's two sisters – was four months old when Gina came to work for us. This 'guardian angel' had been recommended to us by our friends the Waldmans in Prato. For her first few days, Gina wore the traditional maid's uniform, a blue dress and smart white apron. However, it did not take her long to realise that she could drop such formality with us. She had come to Rome with her husband, Orazio, from a remote Calabrian village high in the Sila mountains. Orazio's Roman career had started in the *Carabinieri* mounted police force but, after a bad fall from his horse, he had been obliged to give up this glamorous job and work as an ordinary clerk in the Ministry of Finance. They were a devoted couple, and every morning he would drop Gina off in his Fiat Cinquecento. She spoke only Italian, in a broad southern dialect. She adored Emily, having never been able to have children of her own. My mother was horrified when she heard, from Canadian visitors, that all the nappies hung outside our row of windows to dry in the sun – as did all washing in that neighbourhood! Gina looked after us completely for

Emily's christening in the Church of San Clemente, Rome. The church was frescoed by the Renaissance painter Masaccio in the early fifteenth century

nearly fifteen years. When we moved up the Janiculum Hill to a large flat on the Via Dandolo, she came, too, and when the other occupants of this new building complained because we put metal bars on Emily's bedroom window, far above ground level, Gina flew to the rescue and pointed out that we only had one child and could not afford to lose her! After Jocelyn was born in June 1971, Gina used to hold one child under each arm. She loved them as hers. The only flaw in this blissful domestic arrangement was the *ospiti* (house guests). As Gina and Orazio were perceived by those at home in the mountains to be so rich and successful in the capital, they could not reveal to them the fact that Gina was working as a domestic to make ends meet. Thus, when the *ospiti* appeared for a visit, we had to fend for ourselves. Usually this situation only lasted two or three days, but there were times when we also had *ospiti!* On these dreaded occasions, Gina would appear during her guests' siesta hour and give us a hand. When I had my appendix out, she took Jocelyn, aged two, home for lunch and his siesta every day but not Emily, who was old enough to explain who she was and thus give the game away to friends and neighbours. To keep my strength up when Jocelyn was on the way, Gina used to bring me eggs in her handbag, still warm, laid that morning by illicit hens kept on their rooftop. She would make me a *zabaglione* for breakfast, using the fresh yolks, masala and sugar. She would do this for me often in the years that followed, when exhaustion threatened to engulf me.

Those early years were a joy. One could park one's car in Piazza Navona while having a cappuccino at the Tre Scalini bar. John once lost our children at the Epiphany Fair in Piazza Navona and had them returned to him on the shoulders of smiling *Carabinieri*. These were the days of Aunt Margaret (Mather), well over ninety when we met her in Rome. She was a sort of cult figure in the Ormond family, one of the few survivors of the Hindenburg Zeppelin disaster in 1937 and became a friend of the Ormonds through another American, Ilka Feather, who adored John's father Conrad, as many ladies did. Aunt Margaret arranged wonderful drives for her friends to interesting places in and around Rome; Ilka invited us to her beautiful villa above Florence, from which you looked down on the city and felt you could touch the cupola of the Duomo. They were ladies of another era and still lived an almost pre-war life.

Most of our time in Rome coincided with a politically turbulent period. The *Brigate Rosse* were not only bombing banks and railway stations throughout the country; in March 1978, they also kidnapped Aldo Moro, a key figure in the Christian Democrat government (and a former prime minister of Italy), at that moment busily trying to negotiate a historic compromise with the Communist Party. Fifty-five days later, Moro's dead body was found in the boot of a Renault 4 parked in the Via Caetani between the headquarters of the Christian Democratic Party and the Communist Party in the heart of the city. The mass media played a huge role in this unfolding drama – so much so that even our children, aged seven and nine, greeted us with the horrendous news of his murder as they jumped off their school bus. That evening, the whole city was in shock; there was not a sound on the streets. However, in spite of the continual political unrest, daily life seemed to move on relatively happily. We were always so impressed by the remarkable resilience of the Italians.

When the children were very small, we spent a whole summer in a rented house outside Palinuro, a fishing village then a seven-hour car journey south of Rome. It was totally unspoilt by the passage of time. However, when we took my mother there on her holiday visit from Canada, she found it much too 'unspoilt'! The house was without electricity and telephone, and the many terraces were perilously unsafe for small children. Jocelyn became seriously ill with mumps, so I spent hours queuing for the one public telephone to ring our doctor in Rome, leaving my mother completely isolated with the children. On her last day, Jocelyn being better, we got out to explore the coastline. A boat had been specially organised to take us through the intense blue grottoes for which this area is famous. The day was a great success, including a succulent shellfish lunch by the sea. However, as we finally turned the corner into our village, we saw, to our horror, that the whole hillside was ablaze! Feuding families had chosen this day of all days to put a match to each other's olive groves. My mother became hysterical and refused to return to the house. She insisted we all cram into the only available room at the one local hotel for the night. The next day, she gratefully departed, only twenty-four hours before a serious outbreak of cholera was announced in Torre Annunciata, on our side of Naples. The health authorities took it very seriously, insisting that everyone along the coast south of Naples be vaccinated and requiring all the villages to be sprayed with disinfectant. Food was not allowed to be shipped down the coast, so we survived on bread, figs, tomatoes and deep-water fish brought in by the local fishing boats. The children, who did not like any of these things, lived on biscuits for the next ten days.

We loved the South and explored Naples and its environs many times. We were fascinated by the life of the inner city, especially those streets around Spaccanapoli that were festooned with washing and punctuated by huge palace doorways crowned with the family crests of the aristocracy. The basements of these once-grand palaces, referred to as *bassi fundi*, were homes to the poorest Neapolitan families. The name may have been inspired by the famous caves in Matera. One could peer surreptitiously into the bedrooms and sitting rooms and note the very basic facilities. We were shocked by this poverty and arranged to meet the priest Don Mario Borrelli, founder of Casa dello Scugnizzo. He had done as much as he could to save the homeless street urchins, or *scugnizzi*. In order to win their confidence, Borelli had disguised himself as one of them and eventually managed to establish a home for them.[3] We also got involved with the Fondazione Napoli Novantanove, created in 1984 by the Baron and Baronessa Barracco to save the historic aspect of the city centre and the culture of its people. Much of the medieval and baroque architecture had been badly bombed in the Second World War and was still unrestored.

Inspired by Virgil's *Aeneid*, John and I tried to write a literary guide to the less accessible classical sites on the periphery of Naples. Virgil describes Lake Avernus, the crater of an extinct volcano in the Phlegraean Fields, as the entrance to Hades, and Aeneas seeking out the grotto of the Cumaean Sibyl in a deep cave close at hand. His pastoral poetry inspired the romantic subject matter of the French landscape painter Claude Lorrain, and J.M.W. Turner immortalised the beauty of Baiae's Bay, with its ruins of fashionable seaside villas built in the late Roman Republic. This spot was given a place in the poetry of Keats and Shelley. We also included Emma Hamilton's villa at nearby Posillipo, on the basis of her *Attitudes*, her theatrical enactments of famous mythological characters intended to entertain Sir William Hamilton's erudite guests. We found many interesting sites on our research trips but, sadly, could not find the right London publisher. John then embarked on a study of the palaces of seventeenth-century Naples, with a view to a book on their social history. It was on one of these visits to Naples that we decided, lunching outside in the February sunshine with Capri in the distance, that we could not countenance a return to England at the end of our original two-year trial period.

1: The Sargent great-grandparents had left Philadelphia to travel in Europe before the American Civil War and had lived in various cities there; they never returned to the United States.

2: Percy died in 1965. He is best known for his 1921 book *The Craft of Fiction*, which greatly influenced the novelists of his generation and beyond.

3: *Children of the Sun: The Slum Dwellers of Naples*, Morris West, William Heinemann Ltd, 1957.

CHAPTER 18

Roman Pictures

Having moved to our large flat on the Janiculum Hill, we made many good friends at the American Academy in Rome, situated at the top of the hill, initially through our children playing together in the park of the adjacent Villa Sciarra. John and Teresa D'Arms were among the first. John came to the Academy initially as the Classical Scholar in Residence, and our daughters attended the same local Montessori school; he returned in 1977 as Director. John D'Arms was a great supporter of John Ormond and his book on the seventeenth-century palaces of Naples and invited him to lead a tour of the palaces for a group of American Academicians. John D'Arms generously observed that when John Ormond's book on Neapolitan palaces was published, there would never be a need for another: John Ormond would cover all there was to know! It was, however, daunting for a foreigner to use the archives in the National Library in Naples at that time. Sadly, as with the article on the location of Saint Peter's Crucifixion in Rome, the book was never finished. John always loved the research but found the discipline required for writing difficult and, being a perfectionist, was never quite sure that he had found the right solution.

Teresa D'Arms was Evelyn Waugh's eldest daughter, and she shared her father's razor-sharp wit. Her youngest sister, Harriet, an aspiring (and, in due course, successful) novelist displaying the same black humour as her father, came to stay in Rome while writing her first book, *Mirror Mirror*. Teresa warned us, when we invited Hatty to dinner, that we might find ourselves appearing as unsympathetic characters in the plot!

Henry (Hank) Millon, an architectural historian from MIT, came as the Director in 1974. Hank was very encouraging over my efforts to get back into the art history world. He heard that I had started conducting historical tours of Rome for embassy groups and asked me to organise a tour of Sicily for the Academy scholars. It would have been very stimulating, but I could not justify sacrificing so much of the time I spent with my children; they were still very young. Later on, he supported me in my successful application for a teaching post in art history at the John Cabot University programme in Rome, which led eventually to a more challenging teaching role at Temple University Abroad, where I ran the department. When we left Rome in 1983, he encouraged me to enrol for a PhD with Francis Haskell or Jennifer Montagu in London, although, in the end, I never wrote the thesis.

When Hank returned to the United States, he was chosen to be the first director of the Center for Advanced Study in the Visual Arts (CASVA) at the National Gallery of Art in Washington. In later years, we stayed in Washington with the Millons and met a great number of interesting scholars through them – including the art historian Elizabeth Cropper, whose shoes I had filled at Temple in Rome.

Through these friendships and our interest in art history, we were invited to become members of the library at the American Academy, and to the Academy soirées and lectures. We had never heard of the famous American composer John Cage, the Musician in Residence. Thus, unlike most of the audience, when he sat at the piano without making a sound we did not realise we were listening to his most famous piece, *Four Minutes and Thirty-three Seconds*. We were also part of the vast crowd which had gathered to hear James Stirling, one of the innovative architects of post-war Britain. So many architectural students turned up from Rome University that his lecture had to be reorganised in the Academy garden on a makeshift platform, with a double-bed sheet for his slides. It was not unlike the Sermon on the Mount! His subject was the Cambridge University History Building (1964–67). It was all glass and looked amazing but turned out to be too hot for British students on sunny days. The well-known American sculptor Frank Stella, famous for large-scale mixed-media reliefs, was a Fellow one year and, to everyone's disappointment, he only exhibited a large series of white paper doilies. We took Emily, aged eleven, to his lecture on these cut-outs. She was the only person in the room who dared admit the lecture was incomprehensible! Richard Trythall, an earlier Musician in Residence who had subsequently settled in Rome, gave a talk and demonstration on electronic music, which most of the audience had never heard before.

We often met the Lavins at these events. Irving Lavin was the world expert on Gian Lorenzo Bernini and was highly honoured by the City of Rome. His wife Marilyn was also an art historian, writing on Piero della Francesca. In the early Eighties, she opened my eyes to the value of computers for academic research, enabling comparisons on one screen between a number of chapels and their frescoes; in my old-fashioned naivety I had thought computers were only useful for science and commerce. The Lavins spent as much time as they could justify in Rome; Irving used to say that they had to go home to the US every so often just to remind themselves of the 'real world'. I often wondered if this applied to us when going back to Britain each summer. I think it did.

Other valued friends close to the Academy circle were the LaPalombaras. Joseph was a highly distinguished political economist with a professorship at Yale. His particular interest in Italian politics and economics led to his appointment as First Secretary for Cultural Affairs at the American Embassy in Rome in 1980–81. His wife Constance was a painter and working towards a Master of Fine Arts degree at the Tyler School of Art, Philadelphia, part of Temple University. In Rome, she enrolled in the art history seminar I conducted for graduate students at Temple and loved the Italian Old Masters we studied. After returning to Connecticut, Constance concentrated on painting modern urban landscapes; in atmosphere reminiscent of the work of the American artist Edward Hopper and inspired by the fragmented cityscapes of ancient Rome, they are about geometric space and light. I treasure her oil of the Ponte Rotto, which I bought from her at a later date. The subject, the oldest Roman stone bridge over the Tiber, dating from 180 BC, evoked for her both the ancient and modern characters of the city and she manages a fascinating ambiguity between the two.

The LaPalombaras not only cut a dash on the American Academy tennis courts but gave wonderful *spaghettata* parties in their flat. Joseph always introduced lively and challenging topics of conversation on current affairs. I think he was too Italian at heart to enjoy being an American diplomat. He already knew Italy intimately, having spent time there every year since 1952; undoubtedly, he understood it from a completely subjective point of view. He was brought up on the Near West Side of Chicago in the Italian immigrant community and, although first-generation American, Joseph always remained, for us, distinctly Italian. He won acclaim for his book *Democracy, Italian Style* (Yale University Press, 1989), among whose great admirers were the writers Gore Vidal and Umberto Eco.

Apart from Academy friends, we formed a lifelong friendship with the Pasqualino family, through our children's doctor who introduced us one day in her surgery. Barbara Pasqualino and I had children the same age and were both relatively new to Rome. She had met her husband, Fortunato, whilst working for him as a visiting philosophy student from America. Fortunato was Sicilian, born in Butera in 1923. His family had moved to Caltagirone while he was still a boy, and he was set to work in the orange groves. When the family realised how eager for knowledge he was, they raised the money to buy him shoes so that he could go to school. His academic success was considerable, and he went on to the University of Catania to study philosophy. He was particularly interested in metaphysical approaches to Christianity. By this time, the family had prospered and were very proud of their eldest son. Fortunato was offered a position at the RAI, the national public broadcasting company of Italy. He was a charismatic presenter with intense, glowing eyes. At the same time, he began his career as a writer, publishing a number of books and articles. His first book, *Mio Padre Adamo*, was really an autobiography. He was deeply inspired in early childhood by Butera's annual Feast of San Giuseppe, for which he had been chosen to play the role of the 'Bambino Gesù'. This honour remained an inspiration for the rest of his life and was the subject of a later autobiographical book, *Il giorno che fui Gesù*.

Fortunato's contribution to the revival of the traditional Sicilian puppet theatre was another success. This developed into a Pasqualino family enterprise, with Barbara playing a very active role in organising and photographing the shows in the Theatre of San Crisogono in Trastevere in Rome, in other parts of Italy and even the United States and Argentina. Fortunato, his brother Pino and nephew Luigi spent several years collecting the traditional full-size Sicilian puppets and restoring them and their costumes. Fortunato rewrote the traditional stories, of gallant knights – such as the Paladins of the Emperor Charlemagne's court – rescuing maidens in distress, and scenes from Ariosto's sixteenth-century epic poem *Orlando Furioso*. Their first show, presented in the early 1970s, was based on his reworking of *Don Quichotte*. The performances were completely authentic, the puppets being handled with metal rods in the traditional, swashbuckling manner. They were manoeuvred from above and behind the stage curtain by all members of the family old enough to hold them steady. Fortunato was always the narrator.

Fortunato was one of Jocelyn's godfathers, and we got to know the whole family very well, including Fortunato's siblings and their spouses who would often visit from Sicily. We enjoyed years of extended lunches together. The last of these occasions was our farewell to Rome in late August 1983. We left the packed car below, and, after the usual feast, drove away, in tears, to England.

Our other close friends were the Triulzi family. There were five brothers, the eldest of whom, Stefano, was married to a New Yorker, Gretchen; their three eldest children became great friends with our children. We spent many weekends with them at Sperlonga – identified in the 1960s as an important example of a Lazio fishing village. Perched high on the cliffs above the sea, its grey stone and whitewashed dwellings followed the contours of the landscape: some were more like caves set into the rock. The Triulzis were one of many families who bought these houses from the fishermen. The displaced fishermen moved happily down to the 'new town' on the beach. This long beach of golden sand led to a large grotto used by the Emperor Tiberius in the early first century AD.

Stefano and Gretchen also invited us to stay on the Triulzi estate at Colle San Paolo in Umbria. Their daughters Sabina and Monica (the eldest and youngest, respectively, of six children), with Stefano's support, have restored all the old farmhouses, added infinity swimming pools, and run the estate as a very beautiful *agriturismo* near Lake Trasimeno. The other brothers also refurbished farmhouses there for their own use in the holiday months – a nice example of Italian family solidarity. Stefano and his children stay in the traditional large white Tuscan villa near the chapel and the main gate.

In Rome, the children initially all went to the same Anglo-Italian school, Children's Own, set in the rambling grounds of a villa on the Appia Antica, and pursued many other activities together. Outstanding among these was the chance to act in an English-language production of *Cinderella* at the Teatro Goldoni, a small private theatre in Palazzo Altemps near Piazza Navona. The play had been adapted by an eccentric Irish-Italian called Patrick Persichetti. His mother, Mrs Riley, contributed considerable support from the sidelines. She was a sort of Dickensian character, always swathed in 'woollies'. She kept Patrick on the straight and narrow and they lived together somewhere above the stage. Sabina Triulzi and Emily, aged eight, auditioned for the key roles of the two mice who were the narrators. Jocelyn (aged six) was chosen as their understudy and was thus required to attend all rehearsals. The play, a semi-pantomime, did very well at the box office and for its final performance for schools, Jocelyn was indeed obliged to don Sabina's grey velvet costume and step onto the stage. Emily had to prompt him for many of his lines, but the audience happily assumed that this was part of the script: he was clearly a younger mouse! Although our whole life had to revolve round the long hours of rehearsals, it was an exhilarating and novel experience for parents as well, sitting in the shabby, gilded magnificence of this unrestored eighteenth-century theatre whilst Patrick directed the children and flirted with the young Russian pianist providing accompaniment for the songs.

Another great friend was the pianist, Joseph Rollino, who, years before, had also been a Music Fellow at the American Academy. Joe trained as a concert pianist but had found the stress too punishing. He had decided to settle in Rome and gave piano lessons to a privileged few. Emily was one of his pupils from the age of seven, and they developed a close tie – so much so that we lent our drawing room with Uncle Guillaume's Blüthner grand piano for Joe's annual spring concerts. Joe insisted that the Blüthner, which had been bequeathed to John when Guillaume died in 1971, be completely overhauled for the occasion; the expense was considerable!

We had met Joe through Efrem Calingaert. She and her family were very musical. Efrem was one of a few mature students in my art history classes at the Temple University Programme and was particularly intelligent and conscientious. She asked me to supervise her Master's thesis on the Macchiaioli, a major group of late nineteenth-century Italian painters much admired by John Singer Sargent and about whom I knew nothing. Thus we both learnt a great deal!

We kept in touch with Efrem and her husband Michael, an American diplomat, for years and were often invited to their non-diplomatic parties. One of these was to honour the English tradition of intellectual party games, at which I have never scored highly! A game of charades was still in progress at midnight, and I found it impossible to act out for my team a convincing picture of Renato Curcio, one of the founders of the violent terrorist group, the *Brigate Rosse*. It was an incredibly unsuitable subject for any gathering, and the director of the Rome Opera, a great friend of our hosts who was on my team, lost his temper not only because we had lost the game but also because an 'ignorant English woman' had misrepresented 'anarchists as politicians'. He was very angry, and I fled the room in horror. I will never know whether the Calingaerts did not defend me out of sheer embarrassment or because of Michael's position at the embassy. In any case, it was strange that Michael should have introduced such a sensitive subject. The next day, feeling confused, battered and bruised, I rang Barbara Pasqualino. She immediately responded with: 'No Italian male can lose a game of any kind!' However, the director's reaction was, alas, more profound than that. I suspect he was not an Anglophile, and the whole event reinforced our realisation that we could never escape being foreigners or guests in someone else's country, even such a welcoming one as Italy.

The Calingaerts remained friends despite this fiasco, and through them we met another interesting and glamorous musical couple, Ferdinando and Maria Cappobianco. In their penthouse overlooking the floodlit Piazza del Popolo, they organised wonderful musical evenings with lots of champagne. Ferdinando was passionate about the piano and discreetly helped young Russian refugee pianists who had escaped from the Soviet Union. They would come and play for his friends while he worked on getting them visas for America. Most of our fellow guests were Italian.

We met another archetypal American expatriate living, like Aunt Margaret, permanently in Rome. Rosemary Sprehe was from St Louis, Missouri, and her first husband Giorgio had been Italian. The second, Mr Sprehe, had already died when we met her. Rosemary was years older than we were in age but younger than all of us in spirit and very entertaining, with a delightful sense of humour. She lived in the Via Margutta, in a rabbit warren of famously picturesque flats that featured in the Audrey Hepburn film *Roman Holiday*. They had been studios for foreign artists in the seventeenth century – the Dutch painters had congregated there. Initially, Rosemary shared the flat with her equally glamorous American mother, who was also ageless and determined never to die. Despite being disabled by a bad bout of polio in her youth, Rosemary, leaning on her walking stick, refused to be defeated by Rome's endless steps.

My teaching at Temple's Rome Programme, starting in 1977, was a completely unexpected twist of fate due to a chance meeting at a British Embassy reception given by the Purcells. Michael Purcell was the British Minister to the Holy See, and his wife, Julia, a very warm and vivacious friend of ours. Their frequent parties were very colourful as there was always more than a sprinkling of 'the purple' (as the cardinals and *monsignori* were affectionately known). At one of these, Julia insisted on introducing me to an American professor of art history who promptly offered me his job for the following year. He wanted to go back to Philadelphia to escape from his wife, but his Rome contract with Temple had not yet expired. I was amazed and delighted. On the day of my interview with Temple's Director, David Stone, there was some calamity at home but, fortunately, David Stone settled for a meeting with John as my representative. John was a runaway success, and I was hired to teach full-time for one year. However, it went so well that I managed to remain for six years. I had never taught a formal class, but I was left plenty of coloured slides and a few guidelines. It was a great pleasure teaching the Temple students and those from the Tyler School of Art. The two schools were affiliated in Philadelphia, and the Rome programme was very popular for all sorts of frivolous reasons, from weekends at the Oktoberfest in Munich to the leather boots in the shops of the Via del Corso. However, the many field trips to local museums and to Florence, Naples and Venice were keenly attended, and fun. There was the special challenge of getting a group into a church closed to the public, or a magnificent monastic library, or a private palace with two or three exquisite pictures. Occasionally, I had a very left-wing class who hated Roman Catholic churches on principle. It took forthright explaining to make them see that the rich papal nephews, let alone the popes themselves, were often the greatest patrons of the arts!

I made many good friends amongst my students, but Amy Weiskopf, like Constance LaPalombara, was particularly special. Amy was also working for her MFA at Tyler but had extended her time in Rome by nine years. She was a great asset on the many Temple field trips because her enthusiasm encouraged all present to enjoy the Italian Old Masters. She was never bored or tired and always ready for a pizza and a bottle of red wine at the end of another long day. In fact, so ready was she for a party that she organised a surprise farewell party for me and John, Emily and Jocelyn when I left Temple in the spring of 1983 ahead of our return to Britain. When we arrived to wish some of the students a quick goodbye, the *palazzo* was plunged in darkness, but all the students were quietly lying in wait for us inside. I was, for once, quite speechless in their presence when the cheer went up and the lights came on.

As an artist, Amy wanted, above all, to concentrate on still-life paintings and has achieved that goal with considerable success, by adopting the fine brush stroke and intense colour of the Italian Renaissance. She has shown her work in New York and in New Orleans, Boston and California. For those of us who have visited her at her summer retreat in Lucignano d'Asso in Tuscany, all is revealed. Not only is her light-filled kitchen a display cabinet for her vegetable and fruit compositions but the big window also beckons you to gaze on the golden Tuscan landscape. However, she will explain that landscape is a huge challenge for her – its elusive scale is so much harder to convey on canvas. As a family, we have often stayed over the hills in the Val d'Orcia and gone to Amy's village for lunch. The one and only local shop doubles as a *trattoria* and the menu is always just what one wants: local ham and cheese and dripping melons. If you stayed with Amy, she would drive you into Siena to spend the day in the Museo Civico, looking at the fourteenth-century Sienese Masters. Or you might be taken to the nearby sixteenth-century church and monastery of Sant'Anna in Camprena, where some of the most famous scenes were shot for the film *The English Patient*.

Another Temple student who became almost a member of the family was David Schmidt, together with his wife, Coleen Hayley. We met again in 1984 in London, where Dave had enrolled in the London School of Architecture for a postgraduate degree. We had intensive Saturday evenings of racing demon followed by delicious dinners and much hilarity. Very sadly, the good times ended in tragedy. Having been a haemophiliac from birth, Dave had been forced into a life of regular blood infusions. By 1987, AIDS was entering the blood supply bank. Dave became one of its many victims. He fought nobly for a couple of years but could not survive.

John and I felt we saw almost everything in Rome. In the early Seventies, before the days of mass tourism, we were privileged to be invited by various members of the 'Black Aristocracy' to soirées in their secluded palaces. These were the noble families who had sided with the Papacy under Pope Pius IX against the Italian House of Savoy, which, in 1870, overthrew the popes and the Papal States. These candlelit evenings were often centred around a chamber music concert in *saloni* decorated with ravishing frescoes or hung with beautiful pictures. These palaces had throne rooms with large thrones draped in red brocade to demonstrate their affiliation with the popes; the one in the Palazzo Colonna is still a fine example. Exclusive tours of the Vatican Palace were occasionally on offer, as well. We were able to see the late frescoes of Michelangelo in the Capella Paolina, which leads off the Sistine Chapel and is never open to the public, and Raphael's *Loggia*. On another excursion, we explored the sixteenth-century Casina of Pius IV in the Vatican gardens, designed by Pirro Ligorio. Once, we were included in a rare visit to the actual grave of St Peter under the apse of the present Basilica of St Peter. And the American Academy invited us to join them for a privileged visit to the Villa Albani, situated just outside the third-century city walls and built for the connoisseur Cardinal Alessandro Albani between 1747 and 1767. With its extensive collection of Greek and Roman statues, bas-reliefs, mosaics and paintings displayed in a grand setting of fountains, stairways, frescoes and an 'Italian' garden, the villa is a fine example of the antiquarian taste characteristic of the mid-eighteenth century. It was considered an important landmark on the Roman section of the Grand Tour, though today it is never open to the general public.

We also got permission to see the painted interiors of Roman houses from the Republican era beneath the *Fori Imperiali* and *columbarii* (votive recesses for funerary urns) tucked into private gardens abutting the third-century city wall, but these privileges had ceased to exist by the end of our fifteen years in Rome. The Accademia di Belle Arti di Roma, which falls under the Italian

Ministry of Education, has now tackled the problem of managing the ancient sites by making the Palatine, the Forum and the Colosseum into an organised archaeological park. Thus, these places, although magnificent, have now lost much of the romanticism and solitude of an earlier era.

On our own, John and I traced as best we could the courses of the eleven Roman aqueducts, from the Roman Campagna (countryside) around Rome through the gypsy encampments on the outskirts. Most notable of these was the Acqua Claudia, which ran through the mantle of the ancient Roman gateway of Porta Maggiore, into the gardens of the British Embassy (the Villa Wolkonsky) and on to the Palatine Hill.

We got to know the priest in charge of the eighteenth-century Corsini Chapel commissioned by Pope Clement XII in St John Lateran, one of the four major Roman basilicas, and were thus able to enter and admire the magnificent sculptures in it whenever we liked. When I decided to try and write a PhD on this sculptural programme in 1983 for Dr Jennifer Montagu, our friend the priest happily photocopied all the eighteenth-century documents for me. Jennifer, who we thought would be horrified by such treatment of the documents, was delighted to be given the photocopies! During what was to be our last summer in Rome, John had enjoyed helping me to find, and distinguish between, the various styles of the eighteenth-century sculptors in Rome, who were still relatively unresearched. We used to practice our connoisseurship on the twelve large-scale marble apostles adorning the Lateran nave, executed by a number of these sculptors. Despite his prodigious knowledge, John usually preferred the supporting role in our joint projects, and I could not have done without him.

Where were Emily and Jocelyn? Usually with us on the many sightseeing trips we did at weekends. They loved all the Roman ruins, the many monastic communities and the sixteenth-century villas we explored throughout Lazio. The gardens of Bomarzo, with their grotesque giant sculptures and stone follies whose doorways and windows were mouths and eyes in monstrous faces, were a favourite. It was rather like a sixteenth-century Disneyland.

One of the most poignant friendships we had in Rome was with Giselle Waldman. Giselle was very shy and deeply devoted to her mother. When her mother died suddenly of cancer at the end of 1969, Giselle's hair turned white overnight with shock. Fortunately she had many devoted friends and eventually came to terms with her grief. Despite having been brought up in London, Giselle regarded Rome as home and spoke beautiful Italian; she always gave her nationality as 'Jewish'. She lived in a series of tiny, picturesque flats in old Rome crammed with books, and did much to introduce us to the customs of the city, as well as some of its lesser-known corners. She was an excellent cook, and dining with her was always heartwarming. Classical music would greet you as you ascended the narrow stair. We asked her to be Jocelyn's godmother, and at the christening, in the Castiglione Chapel of the basilica of San Clemente, this frail little lady was obliged to hold our heavy baby for far too long while we argued with Father Boyle about 'Jocelyn' not being acceptable as it was not a saint's name. Luckily, Louis was his second name and, thus, the ceremony was allowed to proceed on that basis!

Martin and Jenny Morland were among our favourite British embassy friends. They once gave a party for the Ambassador, Sir John Nichols, who had demanded that he be introduced to their 'bohemian' Rome friends – those who were not on the list for formal embassy receptions. We qualified for this event and, by chance, at dinner I sat next to the Italian sculptress, Fiore de Henriquez, who asked me for news of her old friend Reine Pitman, John's aunt. Reine's husband Hugo had never approved of their friendship, dating back to Reine's days at the Slade School of Art. Also at the party were the French Commercial Counsellor and his wife, Jean-Luc and France Granier. I had been giving Jean-Luc English conversation lessons but felt constantly discouraged as he insisted on using a pre-war English Grammar. However, on this particular evening, he was determined to show me how much he had learnt. During a lull in the buzz of conversation he pointed to a large bowl of punch on a central table and said in a loud voice, 'Ah, Flavia, there is the slop bowl'! It was indeed a slop bowl from a pre-war bedroom washstand set! The whole room turned to gaze in astonishment. I was acutely embarrassed.

I had also taught English to Jean-Luc's and France's four teenage children in the months before Emily was born, when we first arrived in Rome. The two eldest children, Florence and Luc-François, stayed with us during one of our first summers in Italy to help us with the children, who were very small. They accompanied us to Palinuro, where Luc-François, an artist, alternately sketched and slept through long hot afternoons, with Jocelyn and Emily curled up against his back. They were both charming. Florence was very beautiful and Luc-François very amusing.

We met the eccentric Irish peer, Sir Jack Leslie. His father had been Granny's great friend in the 'Men of the Trees' Society, and our introduction may well have come through Aunt Shiela. In Rome, he was recognised as a devout

Catholic and pillar of the Order of Malta. He would invite guests to lunch at his romantic, crumbling monastery just outside Rome. The name of the monastery was Badia di San Sebastiano di Alatri and he had received a papal knighthood for its restoration. When invited to lunch there with our children, we were, luckily, warned about the need to bring lots of food, as his cupboard was always bare.

In Florence we stayed with my beloved cousin, Richard Fremantle, and also on the estate of Bernard Berenson's Villa I Tatti with the Millons. Nearly every Easter, we returned to the once-fashionable but by then slightly faded Albergo Caruso Belvedere, in Ravello. We loved the view from our balconies over the lemon groves stretching down to the sea far below. Gore Vidal had a house in Ravello, but we did not meet him. We did, though, meet Monsignor Bruno Scott James there. He was famous for his translation of *The Letters of St Bernard of Clairvaux*, which John kept by his bedside, as well as for his work with the poor in Naples. He was also great fun and wonderfully irreverent. At dinner, he delighted our children by lighting the ends of *grissini* (bread sticks) with matches, to pretend he was smoking cigars (prompting the waiters to stand by with a bucket of water).

Part of our Italian experience was a farmhouse in Umbria which we bought in 1974 with the help and encouragement of my mother, who used to come every year to Italy to stay with us and to see her grandchildren. The house was reached down a perilously rutted stone track from the village of Morruzze, about twelve kilometres from the city of Todi. This restored sixteenth-century stone farmhouse, complete with an old threshing floor, was set amongst olive groves sloping down to a valley. Luckily, it already had central heating and electricity, but in the hot weather, black scorpions crawled up the bedroom walls. When the children were small, we spent a lot of time there and foolishly thought we could make it our main residence and use the flat we were renting in Rome just for school terms. This was a complete disaster: it was too isolated. There were no neighbours nearby, especially in winter when summer friends had returned to the city. Even our efforts to expand the olive orchard did not make this lifestyle fly. However, we did enjoy the excitement of olive-picking in a dry sharp wind, traditionally on 8 December, the Feast of the Immaculate Conception. The local farmers who picked them for us would sit in the trees and their nimble fingers would fly along the branches. We also enjoyed the delicious first pressing of our own olive oil, which we had watched being pressed in a one-room olive oil mill nearby. We got to know every corner of

Umbria and entertained many house guests, including Aunt Lulu and Uncle Robert. Aunt Lulu caused quite a sensation by falling out of a fig tree into someone else's field and was thus seen to be stealing their fruit. She had to be rescued by the owner, who had been a prisoner of war in Cornwall during the Second World War and was always telling us how much he had liked it there. Another day, she rose at dawn to pick mushrooms. Fortunately, the owner of the local bar insisted on checking her choice of mushrooms, and all but three were eliminated as poisonous. Aunt Lulu was crushed.

Our house was very informally looked after by Alfredo, the farmer who was our closest neighbour, but when late one night some burglars drove down the track, he and his wife cowered beneath their bed covers. Everyone in the village heard their car and shivered with fear. They were convinced it was the dreaded *Brigate Rosse*, who were then so active all over Italy. We lost a beautiful fox fur rug and all our camping equipment, but the burglars were evidently hoping for much more.

We loved Morruzze, but the old wanderlust set in and we did not want to be tied to having all holidays there. We sold it when we left Italy in 1983.

CHAPTER 19

Behind the Iron Curtain

As the children grew older, we began to look further than Morruzze and our immediate surroundings. We explored several other countries in Europe during the long summer holidays, getting more adventurous as the years went by.

Two of our greatest adventures were in Eastern Europe in the summers of 1982 and 1984. For our first trip there, the four of us set out from Rome in our elderly BMW to see Venice and Vienna before plunging behind the Iron Curtain to explore Prague, Dresden, East Berlin, Potsdam and finally Weimar. Venice was a highlight, as ever, and we were invited to drinks at the Palazzo Barbaro, which still belonged to the Curtis family, cousins of the Sargents. John Singer Sargent painted Mr and Mrs Curtis having tea in the closed loggia on the *piano nobile* (the painting is now part of the Royal Academy's permanent collection), and Henry James had written *The Wings of a Dove* while staying there. We were shown James's bedroom and the library.

The Vienna sojourn featured the Belvedere Palace and the Kunsthistorisches Museum high on the list. The Hofburg, then housing the court dress of the heralds and Benvenuto Cellini's famous gilded salt cellar, was also a highlight. These pleasures and several rounds of Viennese sacher torte were followed by an hour's drive to the Czech border, where anti-tank blocks and rolls of barbed wire stretched across the fields as far as the eye could see. This 'fence' was punctuated by watchtowers and floodlights. For once, there was dead silence from the back seat. Despite all our special visas for Eastern Europe, we wasted hours getting across the border. The guards tried to read the passports upside down, which was not encouraging.

We drove on to Telč, where there is a remarkable main square, bordered by Renaissance buildings with both Flemish and Italianate features, each with a distinct façade and colour. However, there were no rooms for the night. The hotels were either closed or pretended to be full. Finally, we found accommodation in a village with an eighteenth-century palace, which cheered us up. Arriving in the early evening, we were immediately aware of the loudspeakers on every corner and the excessive amount of beer-drinking from enormous glasses. The people had no other outlet after a day's work. After a mangy meal of brown sauce containing bits of tough meat, we went to bed. The following day, we drove for several hours to visit the restored Bishop's Palace in the Moravian town of Kroměříž. Here, the paintings included a famous late Titian, *The Flaying of Marsyas*, once owned by the famous collector Thomas Howard, 14th Earl of Arundel (1585–1646), a courtier during the reign of Charles I.[1] Not many pictures were hanging in this lovely rococo palace, but our mission was to see the remarkable Titian, which had been there since about 1673. It never occurred to us that one day we might see this picture in the West. In fact, relations between East and West were already beginning to thaw, and it was shown in an exhibition at the Royal Academy in London only three years later. We were so grateful to our children for patiently sitting for hours in the back seat of the car. I think they were excited by our spirit of adventure. We continued on to Prague. This beautiful city seemed eerily deserted, but we found rooms in an impressive and unrestored *fin de siècle* hotel, the Hotel Europa, right in the centre of town. The atmosphere was sinister and, to our dismay, the once-smart hotel's dinner menu was just the same as that of the previous evening.

Next day, we had the Charles Bridge to ourselves, and countless churches with skilfully carved and vividly painted wooden altarpieces. The castle complex, including the Cathedral of St Vitus, resembled something out of a fairy tale. Our German was not good and our Czech nonexistent, but we made friends with a young restorer at the beautiful baroque Church of the Loreto. Mozart had played the organ there and the restorer encouraged Emily, aged eleven, to play it, too. There was no one to interfere. There were queues outside the only bookshop and a queue for cups of ice cream, but the only other sightseers were a handful of Italians. The food shops displayed neat pyramids of tinned tomatoes and beans but nothing else.

Our first three nights in East Germany were spent in a small town called Bautzen, sixty kilometres from Dresden, where hotel accommodation had not been available when we booked our trip. In Bautzen, everyone got drunk in the evening. They were literally weaving round the lampposts – quite a sight, especially for the children. We drove to Dresden two days running. The city was still more or less the sea of rubble it had been reduced to during the Second World War, and we were shocked. However, we were determined to see as much of the famous picture collection as possible, and the collection of *objets de vertu* in the Green Vaults – both housed in a battered wing of the Zwinger palace complex. I can still remember the thrill of the first sight of Raphael's *Sistine Madonna* and, paradoxically, the horror presented by the mangled bronze railings of the Royal Palace hanging in mid-air – all that was left of the palace after the bombing.

Our next target was Potsdam, where we stayed in great comfort in the Cecilienhof, part of which is now a hotel, and were shown the room where Churchill, Stalin and Roosevelt signed the peace treaty during the Potsdam Conference in 1945. As we were already in the eastern sector, day trips into East Berlin were easy. However, our East German visas were only good for certain dates, and we had been obliged to book our hotels from Rome. No change of plan was allowed. John had to register our passports each day with the police. East Berlin was also shocking: the houses next to the Wall were boarded up, and there were still several bomb sites. John wanted to look for the location of Hitler's bunker in front of the shabby Brandenburg Gate, but the guards were always watching, and our nerve failed us. We were able to see Museum Island and the Ishtar Gate from Babylon housed there, as well as the Pergamon Altar, whose original site John and I had seen in Turkey.

We needed a different visa to visit West Berlin, and only got it by insisting that we needed to change money – something that was not possible in the eastern sector. Our instructions were to drive 60 kilometres round the Berlin Wall to Checkpoint Charlie, the only crossing point for foreign tourists between East and West Berlin. We thought this a ridiculous idea when there was a military checkpoint only six kilometres from our Potsdam hotel. We learned a bitter lesson! Having saved time on driving, we spent six hours arguing our way through this local checkpoint in our inadequate German; the guards even threw the seats out of the car in their rage and frustration. By the time we arrived in the colourful western zone, we had lost over half the day and rushed to the Dahlem Museum to see all the masterpieces from the Kaiser-Friedrich-Museum. From there we went to dinner and then to the Checkpoint Charlie Museum, which seemed to be open even at night. Here, amongst other horrors, we saw the Fiat 500 in which desperate Easterners had managed to escape to the West curled up around the engine or in the boot.

East Germans were, on the whole, very hostile towards us. On another of our outings, we went into a workers' open-air café looking for a simple lunch of sausages and beer. They refused to serve even the children and roughly shooed us out. However, a good Samaritan rushed after us with a quantity of bread and then fled before we could thank him.

Our final destination was Weimar. After a long, slow drive to get there, with the putrid smell of black smoke belching forth from old factory chimneys, we reached the car park of the art museum, where we wanted to see the paintings of Lucas Cranach. As we emerged from the car, John suddenly realised that our visas ran out that very afternoon at three o'clock. We had no choice but to climb back into the car and make for the border. We have never managed to return to see the Lucas Cranach paintings.

When John and I went behind the Iron Curtain again three years later with Jocelyn (Emily was visiting friends in America), the year after we left Rome, we stayed in West Berlin and took the sinister U-Bahn, surrounded by barbed wire and controlled by soldiers, into East Berlin. We also returned to Czechoslovakia so that Jocelyn could guide us through Napoleon's strategy on the battlefield of Austerlitz. He had his notes in a reinforced metal box file; the border police were very suspicious about these notes, and amazed when they realised that the potential spy was only thirteen years old. We then spent several days in Budapest, where the locals played chess on giant sets in the open air. As a serious chess player, Jocelyn was thrilled.

Our time in Rome was drawing to an end. We had expected to stay for two years and had stayed for fifteen. The children had been at an English school in Rome but Jocelyn had not been happy there, so we sent the children to schools in England as boarders. We had originally considered Italian schools for them, as they both spoke fluent Italian – indeed, it was their first language. Emily spent a short time in an Italian state school, as well as in the Mater Dei convent school just off the Piazza di Spagna, where she had learned the Catechism and taken her First Holy Communion aged seven. However, the schools were generally strict and old-fashioned, and we wanted the children to be fully educated in the English language.

As well, my Temple job was coming to an end, and John had reached an impasse with his book. The final straw was our beloved housekeeper, Gina, sitting down with us, for the first time in 15 years, and telling us we must return to our 'homeland' as she was now getting too old and tired to go on looking after us. We knew we must make plans to go. We departed at the end of August 1983, under a cloud. First, we did not want to go, and secondly, some Italians – such as the *portiera* of our apartment building – were hissing at us like snakes over Mrs Thatcher's recent undeclared war with Argentina in the Falkland Islands. Italy had strong ties with Argentina, and the humiliations of the Second World War also still ran deep for some.

There had been very difficult moments in our early years in Rome, when the *Brigate Rosse* were at their most violent. There were also frequent demonstrations in the streets. John, oblivious to the danger, crossed the Trastevere Bridge one day into the middle of one of these. The unrest led to regular lightning strikes, including an embargo on salt and postage stamps. Finally, there was not only the kidnapping of Aldo Moro but also constant threats of similar violence from the Mafia and associated concerns over corruption, which even touched our own Italian friends and acquaintances. One of these dear friends, who ran a successful engineering firm, was put under house arrest in Rome for a whole year in the 1990s, for planning to build a bridge in Sicily. He was undoubtedly the scapegoat for many more unscrupulous people. However, our abiding memories of our life in Rome were full of the warmth and vitality of the people we met and of the city's addictive beauty.

1: Both the Earl and Countess of Arundel were noted for their love of collecting and most especially their love of Italy and Italian art. *The Flaying of Marsyas* was actually bought by the Countess in Italy in 1620. However, after her death it was sold in Amsterdam and eventually became a part of the Kromeriz collection.

CHAPTER 20

All Good Things Come to an End

Returning to England was painful. Whatever the problems in Italy, everyone wanted to be happy and to laugh and to eat well. However humble an Italian's means might have been, there were always tomatoes and olives and red onions and wine! In England, we felt we were expected to fit into a pigeonhole, and we never really did. The weather was often cold and grey and the food bland. Uncle Peter, ill though he now was with cancer and a weak heart, saw the difficulties we faced in settling back into English life and reintroduced us to the Birches and to his friend Diana Colville – although, in fact, we did not really get to know them well until after Uncle Peter's death.

Aunt Paddy had died suddenly several years before our return to England and Uncle Peter was very lonely after her death, although, in reality, he was seldom alone. Christie's, where he had achieved such success, remained in the forefront of his life and he perused every sale catalogue and discussed the price of each lot with old colleagues. To us, he was like the best friend one had ever had, and he also remained a sort of father figure to me. We all stayed with him often at Colby Lodge, his house near Tenby on the Pembrokeshire coast. We loved this late eighteenth-century house with all its treasures and its romantic walled garden crowned by a neo-gothic gazebo, complete with a gilded finial, designed by Simon Birch. It was Uncle Peter's 'Rougham Hall': the house of his Agnew grandparents that he had loved so much as a child. At Colby we were encouraged to consume bottles of delicious claret from the wine cellar, and every meal was a feast. After dinner, we played the gramophone and danced. While Uncle Peter was still strong, we played serious games of croquet on the lawn which he usually won. He referred to the yellow ball as the 'yaller', a conscious Edwardian mannerism which fascinated our children. He introduced us to the William Phillips family at Slebech Castle on the DauGleddau Estuary and to William's brother, Sir Hanning Phillipps, at Picton Castle nearby. It was with them that Graham Sutherland stayed when painting his series of mysterious trees and roots. A gallery to display his work had been built in their woods, but the paintings were subsequently moved to the National Museum in Cardiff.

Uncle Peter and Aunt Paddy had created an extensive bank of rhododendrons in the woods at Colby, and a seventeenth-century Claudian view across the meadow by diverting the stream and adding an antique wrought-iron bridge. When Aunt Paddy died, Uncle Peter had a small temple-style folly built in her memory near the rhododendrons. After Uncle Peter died, Simon Birch designed for his memorial an obelisk on the wooded hill opposite, deliberately placed to be in direct sight of the temple. The parkland, part of the Colby Estate, had been left to the National Trust, and Uncle Peter also bequeathed the gardens around his house to the National Trust. As part of this bequest, John and I were given the option of taking over the house for a peppercorn rent, but we knew we could never perpetuate its magic.

When Uncle Peter was transferred to the Charing Cross Hospital in the final stage of his illness, I met Christian Carritt. She was at his bedside one Sunday afternoon wearing a felt hat with a comical feather and accompanied by a large boy with a bunch of balloons. As I had been asked to limit Uncle Peter's visitors, I politely asked her to leave. She retorted, 'Don't worry, I'm a doctor', and went on feeding him essence of chicken. This was the start of a lifelong friendship. Christian was a beloved and successful doctor with a thriving private practice. At Benenden School, she had shared a room with the sculpture historian Jennifer Montagu, and at Oxford she was in the same college as Margaret Thatcher, by whose unfashionable brogue shoes she was amused. However, like most professional women of her generation, Christian had had to fight her corner against the prevailing male chauvinism.

Christian's twin brother, David Carritt, had been hired by Uncle Peter for Christie's, and it was through David that Christian and Uncle Peter had become friends. David was famous for his incredible eye and for pointing out that the painted ceiling in the Egyptian Embassy in Mayfair was *The Allegory of Venus* by Giambattista Tiepolo. As a result of this discovery, the Egyptian government decided to sell the painting to help fund the conservation of the temples in the Nile Valley. It now hangs in the National Gallery.

When Uncle Peter died in December 1984, just after Christmas, I was devastated. I was deeply touched when I heard how many of his treasures he had left to me. My mother, who had come to England for his funeral, instructed me to lie down on the sofa while she read out the will. There were pictures, mezzotints, china, silver, furniture, large quantities of books and his fascinating photograph albums. John and I made a valiant effort to keep as much of his collection as possible by moving to a large house in Netherton Grove, on the border of Chelsea and Fulham.

Simon and Bettine Birch became extremely good friends to us after Uncle Peter's death. They frequently invited us to grand dinners at the Fishmongers' Company and to merry weekends at their country house, Brantham. At a party at Brantham we met the potter and sculptor Grayson Perry. He appeared one summer's evening looking for their son James, who had a great gift for seeking out new young artists and, in this case, a talented potter who was to become a household name through his art, writing, broadcasting and his alter-ego, Claire.

Simon and Uncle Peter had met whilst fighting alongside each other in the Second World War and had become friends for life. Simon had trained as an architect, but the war had made such a career path precarious, so he went into the City, strangely enough into the stockbroking firm owned by John's uncle, Hugo Pitman. He was highly creative and, outside his conventional job, loved to design summerhouses and other small architectural features for his friends. For Uncle Peter, he designed the neo-gothic gazebo at Colby Lodge, the interior of which was painted with trompe-l'oeil frescoes by Simon's son-in-law Lincoln Taber, an American artist who had studied in Florence with Annigoni. Simon and Bettine's daughter Jacqueline had met Lincoln in Florence, where she was studying painting restoration and where she had helped to save some of the artworks damaged by the terrible flood of 1964.

Simon and Bettine's youngest son James was deeply involved in the contemporary art scene. He and his friend Paul Conran set up a gallery in Dean Street, Soho, in April 1987, where they showed many emerging young British artists and were the first to promote Grayson Perry's groundbreaking approach to ceramics. They also re-introduced the British surrealist Aileen Agar (1899–1991) to a contemporary public. Frail as she was, she presided at dinner after the opening. Above the gallery was the famous Colony Room where Francis

John and Flavia talking to Francis Bacon at the Dean Street Gallery, 1987

Bacon whiled away many hours with his friends and cronies, including James and Paul. John and I met Bacon at several openings at their Soho gallery, and we often found ourselves sharing the same Number 14 bus down the Fulham Road.

James had known Francis through his parents since early childhood. He worked with the Marlborough Gallery to organise the Francis Bacon exhibition in Moscow in September 1988, the first show of a Western artist to be permitted in the Soviet Union since the 1920s. Sadly, Francis, who was seriously asthmatic, was not well enough to come himself but his charming partner, an East Ender called John Edwards, was delighted to represent him and accept all the publicity on his behalf. James decided that we should be invited to 'look after' his parents in Moscow, as he had been delegated to look after John Edwards. A special exhibition space had been created in The Union of Artists' Hall in Moscow, and the queue of visitors stretched for a mile. For five days, we all survived on a diet of caviar and vodka. We were followed round by the KGB, even while examining the frescoes in the dark, mysterious churches of the Old Believers – Russian Orthodox Christians who had rejected Russia's mid-seventeenth-century church reforms. After a visit to Lenin's tomb, tourists were expected to stay in the Kremlin or the Pushkin Museum and, as a last resort, go shopping in the market. John, as was typical, instead wanted to study the iconography of the Old Believers and our official guide was keen to help.

Uncle Peter's friend Diana Colville often invited us for weekends at her beautiful Jacobean house in Cornwall in the years following Uncle Peter's death. Penheale was surrounded by a magnificent garden with a small lake. The house had an extension by Lutyens which provided the backdrop to a rose garden designed by Gertrude Jekyll. In the winter, a fire would be lit in one's bedroom, and in the summer this would be replaced by massive vases of flowers. The atmosphere always reminded me of the romantic historical novels of my childhood, by Violet Needham. A large room in the older part of the house, with a fine plaster ceiling, was hung with an impressive collection of Old Master drawings which had been collected by Diana's husband. They were chiefly of the Italian Schools and included a Fra Angelico. Seeing the drawings was a ritual in itself and was by invitation only. I had never seen the practice of covering each one with green brocade or velvet (held in place by metal rods) for protection from the light. Diana loved music and often played the piano for us but would always invite John to play, too; she tactfully suggested he might like to practice whilst the rest of us dressed for dinner, thus helping him to overcome his shyness about playing.

Throughout this period, I was struggling to find work in London. Due to Uncle Peter's illness, I had not been able to make progress with my PhD. Without a PhD, it was nearly impossible to find a post as a university lecturer, so I began teaching a series of courses through the extra-mural Art History Department of London University, travelling to the Workers' Educational Association in Brentwood one evening a week. My old-fashioned mother was very worried at the idea of my travelling so far out of central London, alone and after dark, so John agreed to accompany me each week, one of his many acts of kindness, and we would share a picnic in the car before the lecture. He would sit at the back of the classroom whilst I delivered it, mainly so that he could keep warm, and the people in the class were very impressed by such a supportive husband. I also taught a seminar on Italian Baroque Painting and Sculpture at University College London for a year, standing in for Bruce Boucher, whom we had known in Rome, whilst he went to Venice to finish his book on Jacopo Sansovino. I enjoyed this teaching post and had in my small group both Thomas Dane, who became a successful contemporary art dealer, and Humphrey Wine, later to become Chief Curator of French painting at The National Gallery.

Nonetheless, we struggled to find our place in England, and it was many years before we felt settled.

CHAPTER 21

In India with Jenny

In 1989, we flew to India for the first time, to spend the Christmas holidays with John's sister Jenny, her husband David Housego and their sons Alexander and Kim, who had just moved to New Delhi from Paris. From the moment we left the airport we found India lively and exotic. There was intense colour everywhere, from the women's clothes to the flowers, from the birds in the trees to the red sandstone tombs and forts. On that first morning in Delhi, David took us to see the imposing tomb of the sixteenth-century Mughal emperor Humayun, which was just round the corner from their house. On Sunday, in quaintly English fashion, we all went to the Gymkhana Club for lunch and sipped our drinks next to Lady Willingdon's swimming pool, with its 1930s inscription. Her husband had been Governor of Madras, like Mountstuart Grant Duff, and then Viceroy.

Through my old friend from Cairo days, Salman Haidar, now at home in Delhi, we met Iqbal Singh, who had known Aunt Shiela and Granny since before the war and whom I had met many years before at Granny's house in Mulberry Walk. We had dinner at the Indian Congress Club, the first of many meals there.

After an Indian version of an English Christmas, which began with vivid garlands of marigolds being placed around the necks of all members of the household including the staff, we flew to Bangalore. John, Emily, Jocelyn and I had not been prepared for any Indian town to look so much like England and were rather disappointed. We found a driver to take the four of us to an old sixteenth-century fort in the desert, over unbelievably rough roads, whilst Jenny and family soaked up the sun by the pool in our grand hotel. We did not get back for dinner until after dark, and Jenny was not pleased! She was chiefly worried because we had taken a great risk in plunging off on our own with so little experience of the country. The following day, we set off for Srirangapatna and then Mysore before we turned north to Hampi. The trip took a week. We drove in two old-fashioned Ambassador cars, stopping to look at temples and palaces wherever we went. We covered most

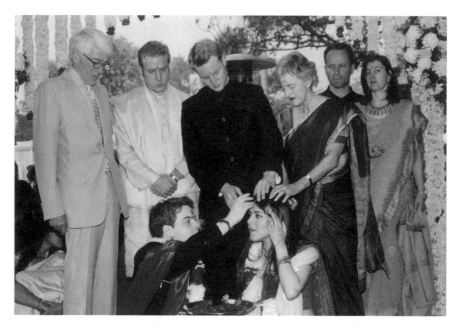

The blessing at Alex Housego's and Abha's wedding in a Delhi garden (back row l-r: John Ormond, Jan-Malte Strijek, Kim Housego, Flavia and Spencer and Emily Cozens)

of Karnataka, staying in fairly unsavoury hotels and living largely on *masala dosas*. One night, in an old colonial-era guesthouse, we were forced to rent the bed linen and all sleep in one large room lit by a single dim light bulb hanging from the centre of the ceiling. In the only hotel near Hampi, Jenny insisted they rewash all our sheets. The colour did not improve but at least one dared get into bed!

Srirangapatna, a fortified island in the Kaveri River, was the site of the Battle of Seringapatam (1799), a siege which established British supremacy in southern India. Every child who goes to the V&A knows of Tipu's Tiger, a mechanical, lifesize model tiger shown mauling a European soldier. This once belonged to Tipu Sultan, the Tiger of Mysore, who was killed in this battle. Inside the tiger is an organ which, when operated, was intended to sound like the dying moans of the hapless European.

Hampi, on the Deccan Plateau, is a vast and still remarkably complete (although long-deserted) medieval city where every building and every artefact is carved out of stone. Dating back to the fourteenth century, it was the capital of the Hindu Vijayanagar Empire, and we spent two very full days exploring it.

We returned to India several times to stay with Jenny and her family, most memorably on the occasion of Alexander's marriage to Abha, a cousin of the Haidars whom he had met in London. It was a traditional Hindu wedding that incorporated Farsi rituals, in honour of Abha's mother. Three days of feasting led up to the wedding itself, in beautiful sunshine just before Christmas, 2003.

Jenny put us up at the old-fashioned Gymkhana Club, and Abha presented Emily and me with saris for the wedding ceremony, as well as a 'handmaiden' to help us put them on. At the henna party on the first evening, the ladies in the extended family had their hands beautifully decorated with henna, which remained unfaded throughout the celebrations. The only part of the tradition not followed was the bridegroom's arrival at the wedding on an elephant. Alexander flatly refused!

The Haidars came to regard us as almost family after this. We met often in Delhi, and in London when Salman was High Commissioner for India. For his seventieth birthday, he wanted to reunite his old friends in India. He arranged a trip to the foothills of the Himalayas which included us and Phillip Ward Green, my old friend from Egypt now living in England. Phillip, Salman and I had become such good friends in Cairo and had been brought together again through Jenny and David's subsequent friendship with both Philip and Salman in Tehran, where David was working as a correspondent. Kusum, Salman's wife, a well-known actress in India, came with us on this adventure, although 'roughing it' was not really her scene. We set off from warm Delhi armed with sweaters against the cold of the mountains. At one stage on the journey, Salman spied men poaching fish in the river. He stopped the car and chased them away in a rage. He was a caring and responsible civil servant, and the Indian papers were then full of reports about the threats to all wildlife, not just tigers. In the evening, we arrived at a large mountain house, borrowed from an old friend of Salman's, and spent an unforgettably cold night, although wood fires were lit in all the grates the moment we arrived. After a good dinner, we all repaired exhausted to our rooms. The bedroom fires had been stoked up but, nevertheless, John and I had to put the woollen floor carpet over our bedding and sleep wrapped in each other's arms. We had not seen the white peaks of the Himalayas because we had arrived after dark, so the following morning we were staggered by their height and their remote beauty. The effect of range after range extending as far as the eye could see was thrilling. Salman was so delighted by our reactions! After breakfast, pails of boiling water were carried one by one to an outhouse and were more or less poured over our exposed bodies – a primitive and wonderful shower! That day we visited a magnificent bird sanctuary. The birds were stunning in size and colour. On the final day of the trip, John – like his nephew Alexander – flatly refused to ride on an elephant for a trek to glimpse a tiger. One of the sympathetic guides offered to give him a ride in the jeep, and, of course, only they saw the tiger! Those who had politely accepted the uncomfortable elephant option were not best pleased.

Our final trip to India took place after Jenny had been very ill, so it was a simpler trip during which, nevertheless, the vividness of India dazzled us once again.

CHAPTER 22

Flavia Ormond Fine Arts

After Uncle Peter's death in 1984, I had tried to follow in his footsteps as a collector. However, having acquired an oil sketch by Edward John Poynter, part of a group of Greek mythological subjects for which my uncle also had a sketch, I became painfully aware that this pursuit would not fit my purse. Fortunately, my interest in collecting had given me the opportunity to meet the much-loved art dealer, Jack Baer. Jack had enthusiastically introduced me to many collectors in London including John and Charlotte Gere, who in the 1950s had established a significant new trend for collecting small open-air oil sketches. Since the seventeenth century, these had been executed by European artists eager to make studies in real landscape before creating the finished paintings in their studios. John and I were invited to one of Jack Baer's renowned lunches at Hazlitt Gooden & Fox, where I fell in love with a large, voluptuous Neapolitan baroque painting hanging in the main gallery. The subject was *Joseph and Potiphar's Wife*, an early work by the painter Francesco Solimena and just the sort of picture I had always longed to own. Of course I could not afford to buy it, but Jack, along with his partners, John Morten Morris and Niall Hobhouse (a cousin of mine), were delighted to exchange it for Uncle Peter's signed and dated painting by the seventeenth-century Dutch artist Melchior d'Hondecoeter, a medley of birds being a more popular subject among British collectors at this time. The Solimena illustrates a scene from the book of Genesis in which the wife of Potiphar, captain of Pharaoah's Bodyguard, tries to lure her husband's trusted servant Joseph, into her bed. Painted circa 1690, its sensuous appeal could be enjoyed as secular art in a palace salon, despite its moral message. Thus, Solimena and his workshop had been commissioned to paint several versions in varying sizes. Having done considerable research to ensure that my proposed acquisition was the first version, I relaxed and went ahead with the exchange.

It was not until several years later, in the autumn of 1991, that Uncle Peter's lawyer and chief executor, Hugo Southern, unexpectedly invited me to lunch and informed me that a bank account belonging to my uncle had just surfaced in Switzerland. Knowing that I longed to collect and that I was also looking for a new career in the London art world, he proposed that I use it to set up a company to deal in Old Master Drawings – not paintings, as they would be too costly to move around, let alone store. He suggested I go home and ponder the idea for twenty-four hours. I had absolutely no business experience, but the thought of competing in the sale rooms appealed to my competitive spirit and yen for excitement. As an Agnew descendant, dealing was in the blood, and I reckoned I could manage. A solution to my desire to continue as a collector had been presented by Hugo's glad tidings, and I could now afford to buy and sell as if constantly refining a private collection, while turning my hand to the business of dealing. I had always loved playing the changes in life; having been introduced to an enthusiastic accountant, I turned my face to the wind.

What was unforeseen was the attitude of my uncle's stockbroker, who assumed that the money would be his to invest. Here was another case of that time-worn male chauvinism still rearing its depressing head at the end of the twentieth century. In an unforgettable boardroom meeting with all the executors on side, the stockbroker announced that he would allow me to have a fraction of my inheritance (to be frivolous with, as he saw it). I was aghast, enraged, and, to everyone's amazement, burst into tears. There was dead silence in the room, but as a result of my passionate reaction, I won, and we adjourned to the dining room for lunch. My uncle's reputedly tough accountant was amongst this all-male group. Under cover of the joviality produced by the wine, he turned to me and said, 'I felt so sorry for you in there and admire you for sticking to your guns.'

Relying on my Courtauld-trained eye, I began to acquire stock and to advertise in the *Burlington Magazine* and the *Art Newspaper*. It was imperative that I visit the print rooms in museums across Britain and elsewhere, because when I was at the Courtauld, the focus had been on the connoisseurship of painting; recognising styles in drawing, by the same masters, was a different skill. I also began to make a completely new set of friends through bidding at auction. The camaraderie in the London/New York/Paris dealing world stood me in good stead for the rest of my life, as has the privilege of meeting a wide range of drawings curators.

Flavia Ormond Fine Arts opened in 1991 with the support of John and of Simon Birch, Uncle Peter's friend. John invested generously in the company and Simon advised shrewdly on the business side.

We all learnt about the pressing need for export licences. John also worked

FOFA directors lunching in Rome

extensively on the research for the fourteen catalogues we published together in almost twenty years of dealing. Simon had retired from stockbroking and had joined Christie's in order to open an office for them in the City. He loved clinching a deal and introduced us to a circle of prospective buyers.

When I started dealing, John Gere asked me, 'Why would you give up collecting, which brings you so many friends?' Like many others, he assumed that I had more funds for collecting than I actually did. However, with time, I saw what he meant: as a dealer, one could sometimes become, at least for a time, an unpopular rival. John Gere had already retired as Keeper of Prints and Drawings at the British Museum, so, when I started buying stock for my company, Charlotte encouraged him to help me with the attribution of my sixteenth-century Italian drawings. I still own the oil sketch on paper by Cristoforo Roncalli, better known as *Il Pomarancio*, which he connected to a British Museum drawing for the interior of the dome of the Basilica of Loreto, in Le Marche, Italy.

Who were the collectors? In the early 1990s, the market for Old Master Drawings was principally in America and most especially in New York. The January sales at Christie's and Sotheby's created an opportunity for all private

A Selection of FOFA Catalogues

dealers to have their own exhibitions in the city. John's brother Richard gave me an introduction to his great friend Warren Adelson, the leading dealer in John Singer Sargent. They were working together to produce a complete *catalogue raisonné* of the artist's work. Having looked enthusiastically at photographs of my current stock of drawings, in January 1994, Warren offered me a chance to exhibit in his new gallery at the Mark Hotel in the fashionable Upper East Side. He and his wife Jan, who loved throwing parties, gave a dinner after the private view, to which about 40 supporters were invited, including John, Emily and Jocelyn, who had flown out for the opening. I did not sell very much that first year, but Warren had put me on the map.

Until 2008, I continued with this annual event and the Adelsons continued their generous parties and good advice. Warren bought a drawing each year, which was gratifying, as he had such a discerning eye. He also introduced me to one of my best clients, the collector Nina Zilkha from Houston, Texas. I was impressed by her classical taste, which was in bold contrast to her husband's passion for contemporary works of art. His collection was displayed in a separate wing of their splendid house, which was inspired by a French seventeenth-century chateau.

When I started dealing in New York, my mother got in touch with her old friend Jane Blaffer from Houston, on my behalf. We had met the whole Blaffer family when we arrived in Cobourg with Aunt Lulu and the Boyle cousins in the summer of 1940. They were delightfully cosmopolitan and flamboyant, with a romantic holiday house modelled on French medieval monastic architecture, looking out to Lake Ontario in the distance. We children loved going there for scones and jam, and for rides in the pony trap with Jane, who was our mother's age. We were also fascinated by Jane's mother, Sarah. Always referred to as 'Old Sadie Blaffer', she hovered in the background, eccentrically dressed in a belted black soutane, probably designed by Dior. Sadie had married a Texan oil baron who took her to Paris on their honeymoon. Entranced by the magnificent paintings in the Louvre, she decided that the people of Houston must have the same opportunity to enjoy Old Masters. She found a dealer she trusted in New York and, on his advice, bought many paintings which later formed the core of the collection in the Fine Arts Museum in Houston. Her heart was in the right place, although her eye was not fully attuned. Viewing these pictures today, one feels that the dealer could have given her better guidance.

John and I stayed with Jane Blaffer in Houston. On our first evening, jet-lagged as we were from flying the Atlantic, she plied us with margaritas and encouraged us to swim in her outdoor swimming pool. It was February, and the experience was delicious. She took us to see various interesting collections including Renzo Piano's newly completed Cy Twombly Museum. Although he lived in Rome, we had never heard of this artist, who was a contemporary of Robert Rauschenberg and Jasper Johns. As ever, we were out of our depth with the contemporary art scene, but John was surprisingly enthusiastic about Mark Rothko's funerary chapel painted in various shades of black. Jane also extended an invitation to stay in her 'sculpture village', a meditation centre in Indiana. However my mother's firm advice had been to decline; she had tried it and found it very lonely, as Jane would recede into another world. Jane inevitably knew Nina and Michael Zilkha and invited them to her house to see us when she discovered we knew them through my dealing in New York.

Beginning in 2002, Warren offered me a number of Sargent's finished pencil drawings, as well as some rough sketches, to sell on consignment. I was disappointed not to make more sales, but collectors of works on paper were not so interested in Sargent's pencil sketches: they wanted his signed charcoal portraits or his watercolours. However, one of my most enthusiastic New York clients, the collector Diane Nixon, bought a Sargent drawing of a fisherman executed in brown ink to add to her legendary collection of Old Master and modern drawings. She became a great friend and introduced me to the New York City Ballet and Balanchine's distinctive choreography.

Another of my favourite collectors was Kasper. We met through his wife, Sandra, who had already bought from me a drawing by the seventeenth-century Italian artist Salvator Rosa. He invited John and me to stay in his elegant flat on 64th and Madison Avenue, where wonderful drawings by Picasso and Matisse hung alongside a drawing called *Clock*, executed in 1968 with gunpowder on paper by the pop artist Ed Ruscha, whose work we did not know. At around the time we met him, Kasper was embarking on a collection of sixteenth-century Italian mannerist drawings. They shared a room with an enormous work by the American abstract expressionist painter Helen Frankenthaler, which she had given to him as a birthday present. He habitually spent weeks making up his mind what to buy but never made mistakes. In all the years I knew him, he bought only one drawing from me, *Saint Paul Raising Eutychus* by the sixteenth-century Italian artist Il Trometta. I never knew why he chose this one by a lesser-known artist, with its rather obscure biblical subject, above all the others I offered him.

Our friendship was based on sharing friends, dinner parties and going to concerts and the theatre together. Kasper's first name was Herbert, but he was always called 'Kasper', both personally and professionally. He was a well-known dress designer, but, initially, I had no idea. I was surprised that, on short acquaintance, he overtly looked me up and down and commented on my clothes. I found it positively forward and mentioned it to a friend who taught at the New York Institute of Fashion. Without a word she pulled a tome from her bookcase, and there he was! He had launched his career with women's suits, promoted at Saks Fifth Avenue in the Seventies at a time when women's professional careers were really taking off. He loved John and envied him his natural slim elegance. He gave him ties he had designed. When he came to view my shows at Adelson Galleries, he always arrived five minutes before closing time and crept silently round the walls from drawing to drawing with his brown felt trilby pulled down over his eyes. Warren was very amused and used to say he never imagined that Old Master drawings drew such eccentric clients.

The guest list for the annual dinners was always headed by Charles Ryskamp, an expansive and popular figure. Having been director both of the Morgan Library and the Frick Collection, he had very discerning taste and it was a treat to go to his apartment and enjoy not only a delicious dinner, but also the delightful range of drawings on every wall. Charles was, above all, fun to be with. He used to take me shopping at Etro in Madison Avenue and decide which shirt or jacket I should choose for the next New York event. I was to foot the bill, whatever the price.

The collector who consistently refused invitations to the Adelson dinner was Woody Brock. He would create an excited drama at the opening, questioning the attribution of each drawing, and then noisily sweep out! He lived in New York in a tiny apartment bursting with eighteenth-century French furniture (now in the Museum of Fine Arts, Boston) and, in Massachusetts, in a large house attached to an old slate quarry which formed a natural swimming pool. He once invited me for the weekend with the interior decorator Nancy Pierrepont and a fellow Old Master drawings dealer and friend of mine, Mark Brady. Mark persuaded Woody to drive us all to the Sargents' family house in Gloucester, Massachusetts, now a museum, where I was delighted to find the signature of Reine Pitman – John's aunt and Sargent's niece – in the guest book. On the Saturday night, he gave a huge dinner party for us to meet all the Winthrops and the Peabodys, the crème de la crème of old Boston society, as he firmly pointed out. After dinner, he rose to his feet, made a speech, and then sat down to play Mozart on his piano. He performed reasonably well, but when he paused, the guests rose in one body and left. It must have been the customary routine. The next day, he proudly showed us the house where he had grown up. Lunch followed, eaten with close friends and cousins.

Woody bought a large number of drawings from me over the years and once rang me up on Christmas Day to discuss what he should buy from my latest catalogue. He left an imperious message demanding an immediate response, which I felt compelled to give. Emily and Jocelyn were incensed, but this was typical of Woody. He once invited himself to lunch at our house in Netherton Grove; luckily, he approved of the lunch and the setting. To my dismay, he later sold nearly all the drawings he had bought from me through a fellow dealer. He hated it when I started dealing in contemporary drawings; I think it threw his confidence in my taste. I was fond of him and was rather hurt when our relationship faded away, so I was very touched when he rang, many years later, to say how sorry he was about John's death.

I learnt much from Warren Adelson himself. He played for high stakes as a dealer, and seldom failed to win. In order to show my appreciation for all he had done, I kept a sharp eye out for undiscovered paintings by Sargent. This led to a chance encounter with the full-length portrait of Tiny Huth-Jackson, elder sister of my grandfather Adrian Grant Duff, in a penthouse on Fifth Avenue. My cousin Richard Fremantle, Tiny's grandson, invited John and me to meet its owner, Sheila Sony, one morning after my first opening in 1994. We were ushered into a large sitting room where this particularly impressive portrait hung on the principal wall. Richard introduced John as the great-nephew of the painter, and me as the great-niece of the sitter. Sheila was fascinated! Eventually, she decided to sell, and Warren was there to help. He had known of the portrait through the Sargent literature but had no idea that it was just up 5th Avenue.

Elizabeth Oustinoff, gallery director at Adelson Galleries for many years, also became an invaluable friend and mentor. We are still in close touch, and I stayed with her recently on the small Greek island of Sifnos, in the Cyclades where we explored many of its enchanting 365 churches. They come in all shapes and sizes, perched on the hills and lurking in the valleys.

Elizabeth and Warren, together with John's brother Richard and the art historian and Sargent scholar Elaine Kilmurray, are recognised as the world experts on Sargent attributions.

Showing drawings in New York led to many other close friendships with dealers, such as Mark Brady. Mark generously introduced me to many people in both New York and Maine, where he had built a large and beautiful modern house overlooking Mount Desert Island. He loved giving house parties and taking his guests out in an old whaler to explore the islands. Curiously, in the 1970s, Mark had spent a year in Rome staying at the Monastery of Sant'Anselmo on the Aventine. We had been living in Trastevere at the time but had never knowingly rubbed shoulders.

My first sale – *The Ecstasy of the Blessed Giacinta Marescotti* by Giuseppe Passeri

Among our mutual friends were Bill Griswold and his partner, Chris Malstead. Bill is now a distinguished director of the Cleveland Museum, but early in his career, as the chief Old Master Drawings curator at The Metropolitan Museum in New York, he bought the first drawing I ever sold, *The Ecstasy of the Blessed Giacinta Marescotti* by Giuseppe Passeri, a preliminary drawing for an important seventeenth-century altarpiece in a religious college at Viterbo, just north of Rome. For me, Passeri's orange washes and white highlights were a major discovery.

However, looking back on twenty years of dealing, I realise that my enthusiasm also stemmed from the fact that he was simply one of many artists who were new to me. I had never concentrated exclusively on the connoisseurship of drawings before, and I learnt to recognise many artists whose fame had been won in the side chapels of Italian churches.

Bill and I habitually made fish risottos together while staying with Mark in Maine. We poured in as much wine as broth and spent hours stirring, to the merriment of all those present, including the New York collector Diane Nixon.

The shows at Adelson Galleries led to invitations to participate in the New York Art Fair in May and the Salon du Dessin in Paris every March.

This, in turn, gave me an entrée at home in London, where Deborah Gage offered me space in her Old Bond Street gallery for the Old Masters Sales

At the Salon du Dessin with Jay Weissberg

Week every July. I was now a stone's throw from Agnews. Gay Naughton, who was the Agnews drawings expert, became one of my dearest friends. It was a great sadness for many when she died of leukaemia in 2017. Her funeral at the Farm Street Catholic Church off Berkeley Square was packed with devoted dealer friends.

All of these events were made smoother by my devoted team of assistants. I had met Frank Dabell in Rome many years before, at his cousin's chic beauty salon on the Via Sistina at the top of the Spanish Steps. As a family, we went there for haircuts. One day, Frank was on duty at the front desk as a favour to his cousin, and when I deposited my pile of art history books in front of him while I paid my bill, he asked if I was enjoying the *Guide to Baroque Rome* by Anthony Blunt. I was completely disarmed until Frank explained, with his characteristic modest charm, that he was an art historian. Years later in New York, when he was working for the Italian dealer Piero Corsini, he introduced me to his partner, Jay Weissberg, today a leading authority on the history of early silent film and a well-known film critic. They moved to Rome and John and I spent many summers exploring Tuscany with them. Frank coincidentally stepped into my teaching shoes at the Temple University Abroad Rome programme.

I also met Pamela Talese, through a chance conversation at a dinner party in New York. She had been working for a smart interior decorator but gave up that glamorous world to pursue a much tougher career as an artist. She agreed to work for me at Adelson, alongside Frank's partner, Jay. I knew nothing of the famous Talese family but was soon enlightened by John's cousin Larry Hughes, a New York publisher and husband of Reine Pitman's daughter, Rose. Pamela's father Gay Talese, a well-known contemporary author in New York, grew up in the southern Italian immigrant community in Ocean City, New Jersey. He joined the *New Yorker* as a young writer and through it met his wife, Nan, a distinguished editor and publisher for Random House who looked after British writers such as Antonia Fraser, John Crace and Ian McEwan. Nan was famous for the elegant design of her books, choosing different styles of paper and typeset to make each book unique. She presented me with many of the proof copies. Gay and Nan were very generous and once agreed to Pamela throwing a birthday party for me in their smart townhouse. Pamela also became very involved with the Century Club, the famous New York literary and artists' club, and we all used to gather there for martinis and oysters. They were altogether a very lively family. Gay's book, *Unto the Sons*, which described his family background, caused a considerable stir in the New York social world.

Like her mother Reine Pitman (Violet Ormond's fifth child), John's cousin Rose – who lived in New York – had been brought up with pictures; like the rest of her family, she had a very good eye. Rose and her husband Larry Hughes were very loyal supporters and came to all the Adelson dinners. Rose always sat next to Warren, whom she knew well through the Sargent connection. I was most flattered when she bought two landscapes in watercolour from me.

Another stimulating New York experience was meeting the collectors Gilbert and Ildiko Butler. Gilbert had a mind that moved like quicksilver and was a very generous patron of the arts. They invited me to go skiing with them for the weekend in upstate New York. I had not realised that this also meant the luxury of a private plane. For the skiing, I was fitted out from their extensive stock of guest ski clothes, boots and skis. Gilbert took me on a test run, and to my chagrin I immediately fell over and could not get up without assistance. It was obvious to Gilbert that my standard of skiing was considerably inferior to theirs. On the first day, I was left to practice on his farm, around the paddocks enclosing his Peruvian llamas and flock of Hereford sheep. I had never seen such a curious combination of animals, now quite commonplace. Skiing was followed by a ride in an old-fashioned horse-drawn sleigh. It was almost too good to be true. On subsequent visits we often looked at Gilbert's rare books and after dinner we played billiards. Gilbert once asked what our son did. His advice to Jocelyn was to make his fortune first and marry after the age of forty. It was too late for Jocelyn to take such advice, having happily married Phillippa some years before.

When Richard Ormond invited John and me to accompany him and his wife Leonee to Boston for a Sargent exhibition at the Museum of Fine Arts, he also suggested that we make an expedition to Ironbound Island in Maine, to explore the sites which Sargent had painted there. It was difficult to reach, so I asked Gilbert, who owned a summer house nearby, what would be the easiest way to get there. He generously lent us his motor launch, with skipper, to get us to the island and, later in the day, a jeep (with driver) to drive us to his summer house on Mount Desert to see his two Sargent watercolours of Maine. Richard had never seen them. On Ironbound Island, we were warmly welcomed to lunch by its present owners, who knew of Sargent's connection with the island and showed us the spots in which they thought Sargent had painted specific watercolours. Richard was working on his landscape catalogue at that moment.

The Tobeys were good friends of the Butlers but had a more cautious style. They never missed an opening or an auction at Christie's or Sotheby's. They concentrated on Italian drawings and wished to support George Goldner, then head of the Drawings Department at the Metropolitan Museum of Art. David's father had been the cartoonist B. Tobey of the *New Yorker*, and some of his cartoons were on display in their Upper West Side flat. They, too, invited me for a sporting weekend, to Long Island, where I foolishly agreed to go kayaking. The current was very strong, and I had to be rescued from a neighbouring beach by David's wife, Julie, in their car. I felt completely humiliated, whereas I had not minded about the skiing!

Among other exciting New York experiences was meeting the eminent collector Hester Diamond and being invited to lunch to view her ever-changing collection. One year, the dining room was hung with Picasso, with sixteenth-century Italian artists such as Battista Dossi in the next room; the next, the video art of Bill Viola had joined the Picasso, with a sculpture of *Autumn* by Bernini in the hall. Her taste in furniture switched from classical to ultra-modern over the years, often in stark contrast to the artworks. Hester lived with her second husband, Ralph Kaminsky, in a penthouse on the Upper West Side with a spectacular view over Central Park. Ralph had equipped the lower floor with a cutting-edge music studio to which they frequently retired, with friends, to listen to opera. This kind of dazzling lifestyle was becoming a familiar experience to me in the United States. Hester and Ralph also travelled extensively, and John and I once met them coming out of a hotel lift in Bangkok. Like other New York friends, Hester was born into an immigrant family. She grew up in the Bronx, and she and her first husband, Harold Diamond, had begun life together as a social worker and schoolteacher, respectively. They moved effortlessly into the world of serious art collecting and dealing.

I did not know the collector Ronald Lauder, but Sandra Kasper kindly arranged for me to see his remarkable collection in his equally splendid white marble apartment. I was fascinated to see a Jacques Lipchitz Cubist tea service arranged below a group of exquisite seventeenth-century landscape drawings by Claude. This unusual juxtaposition was surprisingly successful to the eye. Son of Estée Lauder, the founder of the famous cosmetics firm, Ronald had supported the restoration of the old Vanderbilt mansion on Fifth Avenue and had been instrumental in converting it into the Neue Galerie, now home to Klimt's *Lady in Gold*.

Alfred Moyer, professor of art history at the University of California in Santa Barbara, bought a number of my more academic drawings. I first met him leafing through the boxes of photographs in the Witt Collection at the Courtauld Institute. He loved making new 'discoveries' amongst the drawings presented for the July auction house sales. Nothing gave him more pleasure than improving on the attribution in the catalogue! He was almost always right and managed to form a fine collection of small drawings – drawings of details, or sheets that had been cut down – by major masters. Sitting next to me at a July drawings sale one year, he goaded me into buying a major sheet by the Italian artist Ferraù Fenzoni (1562–1645) for about three times the estimate and much more than I had planned to spend. Other contenders slowly dropped out, and I found myself bidding alone against a prominent London dealer noted as the Getty Museum's principal bidder. I felt the whole sale room was taking my side: this new alignment of players was making the sale even more significant. There was an intense hush all round me, and I could feel perspiration seeping through the back of my yellow linen jacket as the gavel came down in my favour. My opponent, the losing dealer, did not speak to me again for months: he always bid to win! This competitive experience added to the 'cloak and dagger' excitement that dealing often engendered.

I went to Santa Barbara to visit Alfred, where I enjoyed the warm climate, the relaxed way of life and the beauty of the Californian coast. Alfred's great triumph was an exhibition of his drawings collection in the excellent Institute of Art in Minneapolis, his hometown. John and I flew out for the opening and thus had a taste of the Midwest and Lake Michigan. It reminded me of life in Canada.

FOFA closed in January 2009. We had achieved an invitation to London's fashionable Grosvenor House Fair during the previous summer, but, alas, that summer ended with the collapse of Lehman Brothers in September 2008. Instinctively, John and I felt this meant our luck was running out and that the wisest move would be to close the company. I had already found it difficult to concentrate exclusively on Old Master Drawings (they were getting difficult to find), and an attempt to diversify into Modern British and Contemporary drawings was a major challenge. This combination was recognised as an audacious move by Susan Moore in her article about me, 'Redefining the Line', in June 2006.[1] The stock was there, but I was known for my expertise in Old Masters, so buyers felt unsure about my experience in this new field.

Closing FOFA was a tough decision, but I continued to go to the sale rooms and to see the friends I had made through the art-dealing world.

1: Art + Auction, June 1006; pp. 100–102. 'Redefining the Line', Susan Moore.

CHAPTER 23

Travelling Again

In the 1990s, as travel opened up in more remote countries, John and I decided we must see and understand more of the world. Most of these trips were interspersed between Flavia Ormond Fine Arts exhibitions and fairs and were usually about two weeks of concentrated sightseeing.

One of our most outstanding adventures was our trip to Syria with Emily and a photographer friend, Catherine Barne, in the spring of 1996. Our itinerary was heavily influenced by Jocelyn's travels there four years earlier, on his own, just after he had come down from Oxford. His particular interest was Byzantine history. He had flown to Istanbul and taken local buses to see important Byzantine sites, such as Diyarbakir in southeast Turkey, on the Tigris River. At the time, this area was a hotbed of the PKK, the Kurdish militant group, and we were anxious about his travel plans, which involved taking more buses to reach northern Syria. As he was going to be completely out of contact whilst travelling, he promised to let us know when he had arrived safely in Aleppo. A telegram finally came, to our great relief.

Our driver in Syria, who was from the Caucasus and spoke perfect English, willingly took us in his large Mercedes to wherever we wanted to go. We were determined to visit every site illustrated in our guidebook. Thus, when the Mercedes failed to negotiate a rough uphill track to the remote Hittite temple of Ain Dara, our driver hailed a passing van, into which we all climbed, himself included, in order to proceed on our way. We were rewarded at last by the sight of the great carved stone lions at the entrance to the temple, which we had completely to ourselves. The only way we could find enough time to see the spectacular Roman ruins at Apamea was to explore them by moonlight, with the willing agreement of our ever-enthusiastic driver.

A visit to the pillar of Saint Simeon Stylites was considered by Jocelyn to be obligatory. All that remains of the pillar upon which this venerated ascetic sat in splendid isolation from 425 AD is now not much more than a boulder. The ruined church which surrounds it forms a part of the Dead Cities (dating from the late Roman and early Byzantine periods) in the largely Kurdish region near the Turkish border. We were warned by our driver to be careful because of the bitter political tensions between the landless Kurdish tribes and the local authorities, tensions which were still as intense as they had been when Jocelyn had been there four years earlier. From St Simeon, we drove on to the fourth-century Byzantine basilica at Sitt Al Rum, and then to Refade, where the villagers were indeed hostile and would not speak to us. Nevertheless, no one stopped us as we wandered through the partial ruins of the early Byzantine churches, some festooned with washing, amid the rock-strewn fields grazed by sheep. A shepherd perching on a block of ancient stone played a pipe, his donkey tethered by his side amid a profusion of wildflowers stretching as far as the eye could see. The scene had a timeless quality to it, and, as in almost every place we visited, we were alone with the local people and the ruins.

Amongst my favourite memories of that seemingly peaceful country – tragically tearing itself apart since 2011 – is sitting with Emily in the enormous courtyard of the Great Mosque of Damascus, watching the world go by; the vast architectural complex of the *souk* at Aleppo, largely unchanged since the sixteenth century – and subsequently shattered by bombing; the twelfth-century women's public baths, where I lost Emily amongst the local women in the steam; the Baron Hotel in Aleppo, where both Lawrence of Arabia and Jocelyn had stayed; our sumptuous Easter Sunday breakfast, spread out on carpets by our driver and our local guide in a chilly desert dawn somewhere near Palmyra; and the great Roman fortresses from which we looked down on the Euphrates River, turning into molten silver in the evening sun.

John and I were in Uzbekistan with Jocelyn a year later, at the time of Princess Diana's funeral – we managed to get reception on his field radio to listen to it. The accommodation was basic, but, as a consequence, we felt connected with the everyday life of the country. We were fascinated by the women's fashion of having five gold teeth to display when they smiled. We were driven everywhere in a minibus over very bad roads and stayed at simple B&Bs where we dined on the local staple of boiled rice and mashed carrots. On our first evening in Samarkand, our minibus driver knocked hard on our bedroom door at midnight to introduce himself and plan the route. Although we were all in bed, he seemed unperturbed. Like the B&B owners, he spoke only Russian but, luckily, Jocelyn had studied Russian for a year, so he was able to act as interpreter.

We were enchanted by Samarkand, with its exquisite fourteenth-century blue tile decoration. The Registan (public square), bordered by three ancient *madrasahs*, once the centre of the ancient city, had been recently restored by the Soviet authorities. Whilst having lunch in a nearby café, we met a team from UNESCO who shared with us their concern for the Uzbek government's low standard of craftsmanship – many of the tiles were out of alignment. Nevertheless, the overall effect was stunning.

We drove on to unspoilt Bukhara, where there were piles of local carpets for sale in every square. The textile museum displayed the most exquisitely designed traditional costumes, including women's robes with long graceful double sleeves to indicate the wearer's marital status. Our last destination was Khiva, a walled city straight out of a fairy tale, standing isolated in the flat sandy desert. The dust was terrible. After school each day, the children were required to sweep the streets with primitive, handmade brooms. Our visit to this extraordinary town was marred only by our stay in a newly built guesthouse with unfinished sewers – just having our plates washed in the water destroyed our stomachs for several days.

We had paid out huge sums for visas to visit Turkmenistan for one day, as Jocelyn had read that a ruined city just across the border from Uzbekistan had the tallest minaret in Central Asia. This elegant structure, dating from the eleventh or twelfth century, forms part of the site of Konye-Urgench on the Silk Route, deserted since the 1700s; it is now on the UNESCO World Heritage list, but at the time it seemed very remote. As fascinating as the minaret was, we were distracted by a nearby field strewn with what appeared to be short ladders, used as grave markers and placed horizontally over the flat graves in the desert scrub. Part of our satisfaction with the day was the excitement of seeing another isolated country in Central Asia. We were not far from the Aral Sea and could see serious signs of drought in the thick waves of white salt on the sand, which our driver pointed out.

In 2000, John and I returned to Asia with Jocelyn and his wife Phillippa to explore Iran. Phillippa and I were obliged to buy long black gowns and *hijabs* from a shop on the Edgware Road, and we put them on before our plane landed at Tehran.

Our guide was excellent and was deeply impressed with Jocelyn's knowledge of Persian history and so gave us extra time at every place and drank tea with us in the evenings. The tiles of the mosques and *madrasahs* at Isfahan were extraordinary, and we managed to buy a very fine carpet in the marketplace. The palace at Persepolis, with its deep-cut relief sculpture, was, of course, impressive; but the pilgrimage city of Mashhad was our most exciting experience. We were

Phillippa and Flavia at Persepolis

smuggled into the famous Shrine of Imam Reza, the most important shrine for Shi'ites in Iran, on the feast of Eid. To enter the shrine, Phillippa and I had to wear even more disguise than usual – the full *chador*, like a *burka* without face covering, from top to toe. We attempted to glide slowly as we walked, in imitation of the local women. John and Jocelyn went unchallenged in their European shirts and jackets, despite Jocelyn's fair hair. Luckily, our appearance was convincing enough, and we were allowed to walk through the many courtyards, including that of the shrine itself, and to stand for a few minutes in the doorway to the great mosque of Gawhar Shad. We could see row upon row of kneeling and standing male figures in brightly coloured clothes, and a lot of heavily draped women. This was a major place of pilgrimage, and the pilgrims were from all over the Shi'ite world, dark and light-skinned, rich and poor. The whole scene was very private and very moving. It reminded me of a nineteenth-century French 'Orientalist' painting.

After lunch, we were taken to a beautiful mausoleum, with its variously coloured Timurid and Safavid tiles and its turquoise dome gleaming in the late afternoon light. In the cemetery surrounding the mausoleum, women were squatting over the tombstones which made up most of the paving of the courtyard – a vast, open space. These women, often in groups of two or three, would put the end of one finger on a grave in order to make contact with the dead. A young man came up and offered us dates to eat, in memory of someone for whom he was mourning; it is very important in Iran to accept such offerings graciously. One section was devoted to those who had died in the Iran–Iraq war. Flags, and photographs of the dead men, were arranged on a large wooden frame, but the women who had died in the fighting were only allowed to have their names displayed on a list. According to our guide, 30,000 men and women from Mashhad were killed in this war, many – so he said – by Saddam Hussein's chemical weapons.

The following morning, we were packed into a Jeep and driven to a Silk Route *caravanserai* fourteen miles from the turbulent Afghan border. We were constantly stopped at police checkpoints to have our papers checked. The drug traffic of opium and *hashish* from Afghanistan was a very serious problem, and Iran and Pakistan were both implicated in its passage through the Middle East to Europe. Our guide told us that the drug peddlers came across from Afghanistan at any unguarded spot, and, unknown to us, she had arranged a police escort to accompany us when we got near the border. We passed a military camp along the roadside where a few miserable-looking soldiers were doing their military service behind barbed wire and corrugated tin fences; somewhere on the wall was painted, in English, 'Down with Israel'. The *caravanserai* was down in a dip between two mountain passes, one on the Turkmenistan border and one on the Afghanistan border, and thus had been a strategic stop for merchants travelling on the Silk Route between East and West. Above it, on the brow of the hill to the east, was yet another jeep, bristling with guns. Jocelyn was told that these soldiers were not Afghan but Iranian and were there for our protection.

Our final expedition to Central Asia took place several years later, in September 2009, when we flew to the Caucasus to explore Armenia, Georgia and Azerbaijan. Our plane landed at the Armenian capital of Yerevan, in the dead of night and we were taken to an old fashioned and depressing hotel. However, we awoke the following morning to a superb view of snow-capped Mount Ararat from our bedroom window. It is believed that Noah's Ark came to rest on this mountain after the Flood. Armenia is beautiful – mountainous, with many woods – as are the many early monasteries, small and simple inside. At the Matenadaran Library in Yerevan, we saw the exquisitely illustrated manuscripts from the thirteenth and fourteenth centuries. Sadly our time there was curtailed because our guide was anxious to hurry us on to the nearby Museum of Armenian Genocide. Here the brutal treatment of Armenians at the hands of the Ottoman army, and subsequently the Turkish Republicans (1915–1922), is graphically displayed.

The greater adventure was in Georgia. Even crossing the frontier was a bizarre experience, as our Armenian driver claimed to have run out of the necessary visas for himself and his car. We were thus obliged to walk from Armenia into Georgia, dragging all our heavy luggage unaided, across a relatively long bridge. No one had prepared us for this. We had no idea what lay in front of us on the other side, so we just followed our noses. Fortunately, a young Georgian woman was waiting for us. To our relief, Nino spoke perfect English and helped us to fill out our Georgian visas in a wooden hut equipped with the necessary forms and pencils. It all felt very primitive, but it was a beautiful sunny day and Nino's eyes were as large and penetrating as those of the Virgin Mary in the Georgian frescoes we were soon to see.

Tbilisi was picturesque, but off the main streets one could see the level of poverty. There were not even streetlights, so we hardly ever ventured out in the evening. The Paliashvili Opera House was closed, sadly, but we admired the bronze statue of a dancer outside – a tribute to George Balanchine, who had fled from Georgia to the United States and had gone on to found the New York City Ballet.

Nino was bitterly anti-Soviet. She had been instructed by the Tourist Board to take us to the Stalin Museum at Gori, the town where Stalin was born and went to school. Stalin's elegantly appointed railway carriage, used for travel to the Potsdam Conference in 1945, was on view in the grandiose park surrounding this extraordinary museum and quasi-shrine – as was the tiny hut he had lived in until the age of fifteen. We were fascinated by this disturbing scene, but Nino was deeply upset by our unexpected interest. She felt we were being disloyal to her and to modern-day Georgia. However, she forgave us when she saw how even more passionately interested we were in the ancient churches and their frescoes, and in the beauty of the Caucasus mountain range, its peaks glistening with snow.

Nino looked after us throughout our stay and a week later put us on a train with sleeping compartments for the overnight journey to Azerbaijan. I had always wanted to go to Baku – the name itself was so exotic. At airports, I would hear flight announcements called out for this remote city and feel very dull that we were only listening for Rome or Florence for ourselves. I knew of Azerbaijan only from playing the Geography Game as a child. After a sixteen-hour train journey, much improved by a box of Nino's Georgian sweetmeats, we staggered out into the sunlight at Baku's railway station. Our local guide was a militant lady determined to show us the whole city in two days, and she more or less succeeded. She insisted we go first to Martyrs' Lane, the grim memorial to those killed in the Soviet Army's quelling of the city's popular uprising in 1990. I remember rows and rows of white flat graves against a manicured green lawn. Then she took us to the fifteenth-century palace of the Shirvanshah's, the Arab/Persian ruling dynasty, and to the Carpet Museum with its important collection of Azeri carpets going back to the seventeenth century. However, she failed to get us into the opera house, which was a bitter disappointment, but there was no performance until the end of September, so the doors were firmly locked. Built in the art deco style, with black basalt columns and steps, it was considered one of the most sophisticated theatres in Central Asia.[1]

Driving round the outskirts of the city, we saw small, primitive oil wells pumping away beside the road, a reminder of the oil boom of the 1880s when this basically Persian city was taken over by ruthless Russian oil barons. Their grand nineteenth-century palaces still coexist alongside the twelfth-century defensive walls of the old city. This strange mix of cultures over such a short visit was an unsettling but invigorating experience, as was the view from our hotel window of the brilliant sunset reflected in the Caspian Sea.

We had originally planned to return to Iran in 2002, but after George W. Bush's State of the Union address about the 'Axis of Evil', following the 9/11 attacks, Jocelyn insisted on a safe and interesting alternative on the opposite side of the world from Iran. He suggested Mexico.

In Mexico, we were intrigued by the variety of curiously shaped, flat-topped pyramids – so different from those in Egypt. We were, however, nervous about the large population of primeval iguanas who took their sunbaths on the pyramid steps. I found the Aztec culture rather gruesome, especially after visiting the museum in Mexico City. It is conceivable that the guide was making the most of the human sacrifice angle to entertain us. Otherwise, Mexico City made little impact on our time there, as it was considered too dangerous for us to explore on our own. We felt metaphorically locked into our hotel in the evenings. The colourful Spanish colonial architecture in the smaller towns was delightful, and the massive amount of gilding in the churches quite overwhelming.

This experience whetted our appetite for South America, so we travelled to Peru in May 2008. Machu Picchu, with its extraordinarily intricate Inca stonework, was undoubtedly the highlight. We did not have the stamina to walk to the site up the steep stone steps but enjoyed the mountainous approach to it on the relatively modern train. We were shown the spot where the Amazon River rises on the higher plains but we were underwhelmed:

the spring was just a hole in the ground. However, we were enchanted by the Spanish colonial paintings and frescoes in the churches and monasteries of Cusco. John initially suffered badly from the very high altitude in Cusco (10,000 feet above sea level) and literally turned green within twenty-four hours of arrival. In horror, I rang room service and a waiter arrived immediately with a canister of oxygen, without turning a hair.

My cousin Richard Boyle had given us an introduction to a close business friend living in Lima, and this friend gave us lunch in his grand club and took us to all the finest churches in his chauffeur-driven car – even those not normally open to the public. We were fascinated by the local references embedded in Peruvian Christian art. For example, for the flight into Egypt, the artists often depicted both Mary and Joseph wearing typical Peruvian straw hats as protection against the sun, and the statues of saints were smothered in elaborate, garishly coloured gowns.

We returned to South America in September that same year for the wedding of Jenny's younger son, Kim, in Colombia. Paola, Kim's Colombian bride, and her family rolled out the red carpet for twenty-five English friends and relations and gave us all a fabulous and festive introduction to their country. Initially, we stayed in a modern hotel on the outskirts of Bogotá, where we had to show our passports every time we went in or out. Security was very tight, although we could explore the old town on our own during daylight hours. The FARC terrorists were to be carefully reckoned with.

Kim conducted us all on a tour of the city. The churches were very dark and mysterious. We spent the evening dancing the tango into the small hours and even John's sister Jenny, hampered by the long-term effects of a serious stroke, was swept off her feet. Paola had arranged for the wedding to take place in the carefully preserved colonial village of Villa de Leyva, and we spent several hours getting there in a dilapidated old bus. Founded in the sixteenth century, Villa de Leyva is picturesque, with an unusually large, cobbled square at its centre. The village had to be carefully protected, with armed soldiers positioned behind street corners to protect the guests from FARC or any other guerrilla activity. One could catch a glimpse of these soldiers if one looked sharply. The wedding, in the church that dominates the square, was the height of elegance, Paola's eight bridesmaids in long scarlet dresses offset by the opulent, gilded high altar. The High Mass was followed by a sumptuous wedding feast and party which went on until seven o'clock in the morning. Delicious bitter chocolate flowed from a silver fountain, with succulent strawberries to dip in it, and one's glass of champagne was constantly replenished. At midnight, brightly coloured, grotesque papier-mâché masks were presented to all the guests, some of whom had taken to dancing on their tables, including John's exuberant younger brother, Tim.

The next day, the English contingent flew north to Cartagena, a sixteenth-century Spanish port on the Caribbean coast with impressive fortifications still intact. John and I really bonded with Tim and his family on this trip – partly because we bravely accepted an invitation for a day's excursion in a motor launch to a distant island, rather than choosing to explore more churches. We were all amused by Colombia's relaxed atmosphere, and Tim loved the grand lifestyle of our hotel at Cartagena, where he would hand out piña colada cocktails with a flourish to those lazing in the open-air pool.

The most adventurous part of the whole experience was Mompox – a town described by the Colombian writer Gabriel Garcia Márquez in several of his novels. After another long ride in another antiquated bus, we reached the banks of a broad, overflowing river, the Magdalena. The crossing was perilous, as the ancient ferry was listing to one side and, with the exception of Jenny in her wheelchair, we all had to stand on deck to help keep it balanced. Miraculously, we docked safely on the far shore and got back into our cramped bus. In Mompox, we were taken aback by the massive tangle of overhead wires above our heads, supported by a single telegraph pole. Everyone was horrified except Jenny, who remarked, 'Just like India'. It was very basic, but the surroundings were beautiful. We went out on the river in long wooden boats in the late afternoon. Jenny, in her wheelchair, was lowered effortlessly into one of the boats by three powerful-looking boatmen. We glided past small brown pigs swimming in the dark water and large iguanas puffing away on the over-hanging bushes and rocks. The sunset was vivid, and it was all very entertaining, though eerie.

The next time we saw Kim and Paola was in the early autumn of 2011 in Libya, where Kim was working for Total Oil. They lived in a secure compound on the edge of Tripoli, by the sea. It seemed very peaceful, and I remember thinking the long white empty beach would make a holiday spot for my grandchildren. However, Kim was constantly growling about Colonel Gaddafi's *The Green Book* and how dangerous his dictatorship was. Kim and Paola took us to Leptis Magna, the birthplace of Emperor Septimius Severus who turned it into one of the most beautiful cities of the Roman Empire in the third century AD, and to see the fine Roman theatre at Sabratha nearby.

After our sojourn in Rome, we had longed to see these two ancient sites; they were magnificent, and well-conserved under the Gaddafi regime. Deeply inspired, we made arrangements through Kim, and the necessary 'fixer', to fly to the Benghazi Peninsula to explore Cyrenaica. Despite the fixer, we waited for six hours to board a one-hour flight. There was chaos at the airport, and a very high wind was blowing. The plane was packed, and the passengers were constantly on mobile phones despite the usual flight restrictions. The extensive remains of this most important Hellenistic city of Cyrene made all the effort worthwhile. We found it far more intact than many sites in Italy. There was some very fine sculpture in the museum and, in addition, a plaque and large photograph commemorating a joint visit by Colonel Gaddafi and Silvio Berlusconi, then-Prime Minister of Italy. We preferred to think about Simon of Cyrene, who had been forced by the Romans to carry Christ's cross on the way to Calvary. It was a beautiful day, and our local guide kept telling us how fortunate they all were, as Gaddafi had promised each family a house with land. We saw some of these houses from the road. They appeared to be constructed of very dark concrete and sat on relatively small plots.

We enjoyed being with Kim and Paola, and none of us imagined that three months later they would be fleeing for their lives, their possessions abandoned, bullets flying as their taxi sped from the compound to the airport. The civil war had begun, and Kim and Paola only just got out in time.

There were many more excursions to new places. After my experiences in Egypt and Morocco, I was keen to explore more of North Africa with John; this time, we went to Tunisia. John was particularly keen to see Carthage, and to find his grandparents' house in Tunis. We found the old winding streets of Tunis itself very picturesque and spent time looking for the house at Hammamet where Violet and Francis Ormond had spent a lot of time, as Francis had loved deep-sea fishing. The house was nicely sited on the beach but had become a rather depressing hotel. We loved deserts, and the Sahara Desert did not disappoint, with wave upon wave of pale yellow sand as far as the eye could see. We tried riding camels across it, though John found this a very uncomfortable experience.

On another trip to the Middle East, John wanted to show me Petra, which he had seen on a trip to the Holy Land in 1963. In Jordan, the desert was formed of high dunes of reddish-gold sand. We were fascinated by all the places referred to in the film *Lawrence of Arabia*, which both of us had seen, independently, the year before John's first visit. Petra was spectacular;

entered through a dark, narrow gap in the natural rock enclosure, it was a remarkably baroque experience. One burst forth into a huge, sunlit valley with extraordinary architecture carved into the rock – some reminiscent, as has been noted, of Borromini's architecture in Rome.

We now knew North Africa quite well, so, at Jocelyn's suggestion, in 2012 we decided to fly to South Africa, as Jocelyn thought we would be as fascinated as he had been by its British colonial history. He also recommended exploring a private game park in the north, so we flew to Johannesburg and on to see Victoria Falls, where my father had been so many years before. The game park was quite interesting, but the lions were always half-asleep, and the effect was of wild animals being recycled for the tourist trade.

On the way to Cape Town we had arranged to stay in KwaZulu-Natal at Fugitives' Drift, the holiday home of the South African historian David Rattray, who was sadly murdered by one of his employees in 2007. Rattray was highly respected for the community work he carried out in the area, trying to improve the standard of living for all. His home has now been enlarged into a guesthouse run by his family, who have continued to organise David's famous tours to nearby Isandlwana and Rorke's Drift – battlefields of the Anglo-Zulu War of 1879. We were given an intense tour of Rorke's Drift, and a blow-by-blow account of its defence, by the great-grandson of a Zulu who had fought in the battle. We made extra time to view the site of the first battle at Isandlwana several miles away, where we joined a breakfast picnic party perched high on a nearby cliff, warmed by the early morning sun, that looked out over the battlefield. The site is marked by an extraordinary rocky projection, rising out of the long grasses through which the Zulu warriors crept. Below us lay the spot where the British officers, under Lord Chelmsford, Commander of British Forces in Cape Colony, had been indulging in a large, relaxed lunch when news of the fast-approaching Zulu forces came.

We then drove southwards to sections of the Second Boer War territory where my grandfather Adrian Grant Duff had fought with the Black Watch.

We found Cape Town's tragic recent past very moving. We were taken to District Six, an isolated group of wooden frame houses in what had been part of the now-demolished 'old town', preserved as a museum illustrating the history and the horrors of apartheid. When our driver saw how interested we were, he followed it up with a visit to one of the nearby townships in Cape Flats to which the community of District Six had been forcibly removed starting in 1966. It seemed orderly and well maintained; perhaps he wanted to show us a prosperous township rather than a more impoverished one where our visit might have been bitterly resented.

We were impressed by the exotic shapes and colours of the flowers and shrubs in Cape Town's botanical gardens and admired the formal planting in the vineyards to the east of the city in Stellenbosch where we stayed. There, we found the house where, over a century before, Adrian Grant Duff had spent much time with the Dutch family who lived there while courting one of their daughters.

In 2004, we turned to the Far East, and to China. In Beijing, we enjoyed staying in the Old Town, in the China Club – located in one of the quintessential traditional houses – where we ate the most delicious Peking duck every night. Along with trips to the Forbidden City and the Ming tombs, we walked along a section of the Great Wall, then travelled to the Gobi Desert to see the Caves of the Thousand Buddhas near Dunhuang. This added another desert experience, this time in the form of tall, almost white sand dunes rising out of the disappointingly grey surface of the wider desert. Under great protest, our irritating female guide – who wanted to take us to a Western-style shopping mall she was clearly proud of – grudgingly took us to the remains of the Jade Gate, once a pass on the Silk Road. We were dismayed by the absolute necessity for an English-speaking guide in China: trying to strike out on our own would have been fatal, as we had no language in common.

I found China unexpectedly westernised. Young girls in the cities wore jeans and had long blonde hair, whilst in the various hotels we stayed in, they were loath to wash our shabby travelling clothes because they were 'broken in pieces'. On our second visit in 2006, I was shocked by what I saw as the kitsch in the windows of the main shopping street in Shanghai, featuring Mickey Mouse and bearing emoji shop signs. I could not reconcile this with the beautiful scrolls and porcelain we had seen in the new museum near our hotel; the contrast seemed ridiculous. Equally disturbing was the evening's entertainment in a local theatre, where the show consisted of motorcyclists driving faster and faster inside a revolving cage with a vertical thrust. This crude thrill certainly brought home the tragic effects of the Cultural Revolution and the insidious influence of modern Western culture. However, the Bund on the Huangpu River had been carefully restored and gave one a strong sense of the atmosphere of the nineteenth-century International Settlement, with its banks and trading houses.

From Shanghai, we travelled on to Burma, which had great charm and was peaceful despite the cruel regime in place – we were there just before the crackdown on the Karen Liberation Army in 2006, and the so-called 'Saffron Revolution'. We loved watching the groups of Buddhist monks strolling through the streets in their saffron robes. Our Burmese guide was a supporter of the imprisoned opposition leader Aung San Suu Kyi, whom our friend Martin Morland, a friend from Rome who had later been British Ambassador in Burma, had known well. Martin had strongly supported our trip, although many others in the West did not, because he felt it brought much-needed income to the country, despite the oppressive regime. When our guide realised we were sympathetic listeners, she talked continuously about the repressive political situation and encouraged us to buy textiles and handicrafts from stalls in all the villages, to support the local people directly. We even bought cigars, which we watched the local women rolling. Our guide instructed our driver to go through the modern section of Rangoon so we could see for ourselves the ill-built government housing: cheap bricks held together with gobs of poor-quality mortar. We were shocked. Martin had given us an introduction to a Burmese friend in Rangoon who was active in trying to overthrow the government. The guide would not enter his grim, prison-like apartment building: she must have known she would be watched.

In Rangoon, we visited the deeply venerated and heavily gilded Shwedagon Pagoda, the Burmese equivalent of St Peter's Basilica in Rome. We were also intrigued by the long, low British warehouses, built along the river as recently as the 1930s. We made a two-day cruise on the Irrawaddy River. Our journey upstream ran through a vast fertile delta famous for the cultivation of rice. The delta eventually gave way to a single great river, which at the time of our journey was unspoilt by dams, the construction of which would commence the following year. British colonial steamers from the Thirties had been restored for tourists, and the trip was designed to give one an experience of the British imperial past. The river narrows in the higher reaches, above Mandalay. We could have chosen to stay on the cruise to see elephants moving tree trunks along the riverbanks, but we were getting restless, so we disembarked at Mandalay.

During the cruise, we had been ashore to drift over Bagan in a hot-air balloon. It was a remarkable experience and made me think of Babar and Celeste on their honeymoon, from Jean de Brunhoff's 1931 children's book *Babar the Elephant*. Bagan had been the capital of the medieval Buddhist kingdom of Pagan and the surviving two thousand red brick temples were set into an unending landscape of vivid green trees. We loved all the vegetarian dishes in Burma and were taken in a traditional long wooden boat to see the floating vegetable gardens on Inle Lake. The fisherman sculling our boat was dressed in wrap-around orange cotton trousers, and he took us to see both these curious artificial islands where the vegetables grew and, in a neighbouring lake, a romantic group of small shrines, red brick *stupas* each containing a buddha and decorated with sixteenth-century carved stone guardians and bells. There were hundreds of them climbing the hillside to the main shrine.

Cambodia, in contrast to Burma, had a strange and almost threatening atmosphere. We stayed briefly in Phnom Penh but, much to the surprise of our guide, we refused to visit the 'killing fields' of the Khmer Rouge. We found the prospect too upsetting. The Hindu temples of the ancient city of Angkor Wat were everything one had hoped for. Their design was a combination of Indian and Chinese architecture and many of the structures were embellished with strange tree roots seemingly intent on strangulation – quite a macabre sight.

As well as these adventures on our own, we now became increasingly involved in formal study trips with the Beaumont Group at the National Gallery, which we had joined in 1998. These trips were equally compelling, though mostly to cities in western Europe, and they heralded a shift in my working life.

1: Cf. *Ali and Nino*, a novel by Kurban Said, published by Vintage Books, London, 2000.

CHAPTER 24

The Beaumonts

My final contribution to the art world was becoming chair, in 2010, of the Beaumont Group, a group of patrons at the National Gallery formed in 1994 and named after the collector and landscape painter, Sir George Beaumont (1753–1827) of Coleorton Hall in Leicestershire. Beaumont, like other connoisseurs of his day, had developed his taste for Old Masters on the Grand Tour and had bought, amongst other things, four important paintings by Claude Lorrain. Impressed by the public museums he had visited in Rome, he offered his own collection towards the formation of a National Gallery in London in 1823. His determination to bring art to the general public persuaded the Earl of Liverpool, then Prime Minister, to agree to establishing such a gallery the following year.

The original aim of the group was to follow in Beaumont's footsteps by providing the gallery with extra funds for the acquisition of new pictures. I was delighted to be recommended as the successor to Lady Lever, the founding chair. My name had been put forward by two of my fellow drawings dealers, Katrin Henkel and Kate de Rothschild. By the 1990s, there were many women dealing in drawings, and although we had always competed in the sale rooms and for the attention of prominent collectors, we were nevertheless good friends; our mutual love of drawings provided a permanent bond.

John and I had already been invited to join the Beaumont Group but had not known many of the other members or been able to go on the study trips. At that time, it gave the impression of being a series of cliques, as the founder members naturally brought in their own friends, and, likewise, those friends also brought in people they knew. It had the reputation of being like an exclusive West End club, and we all desperately needed to be introduced to each other. As chair, I was determined to dissolve the rather formal atmosphere and make the events more lively. Nicholas Penny, now the director, whom I much admired, was in agreement. He also wanted the members to focus on the pictures in the galleries rather than on each other and hoped my passion for pictures would lead the way.

After a rather stormy start due to the rigid hierarchy in the Development Department at that time, we got this new trend going. The private views and the yearly study trips became steadily more popular and more relaxed. However, my first study trip as chair, to Venice, was not so relaxing for me, as I had to spend what spare time I had committing to memory the seventy-one names of the members present. My greatest support was Angeliki Alexandri. This dynamic Greek lady, always bursting with new ideas, had already been the Patrons Manager for some time. Over many intense lunches and teas, she and I conceived a new style for the Beaumont Group which attracted a cross-section of younger professional men and women, who looked and listened attentively all day on our study trips and kept the hotel bars happily open most of the night. The study trips to galleries in other European cities had been the idea of Diane Lever and the other founder members, to perpetuate the George Beaumont heritage. On these trips we now shared informal lunches and very elegant dinners in splendid private palaces. Particularly memorable was an evening in Rome where we sat at long tables in the glittering picture gallery at the Palazzo Colonna.

The Beaumont Circle, a new tier for major donors, eventually came into being in 2015, with its own annual trip. A number of the pioneer members of the original group felt this extra and costly privilege spoilt the spirit of equality the group had always tried to foster. It was difficult to make the point that after a period of twenty years, more money was urgently needed to maintain the high standards of the Gallery, whatever the original goal had been. The first of these Circle trips, in a much smaller group which therefore made access possible to collections not normally open to the public, took us by bus from Lyons to Dijon and included the sixteenth-century Royal Monastery of Brou (Bourg-en-Bresse), where Nicholas Penny lectured with great enthusiasm on the tomb sculpture by Conrad Meit. The weather was freezing cold and grey, but everything we saw sparkled thanks to Nicholas and his devoted team of curators. For me, Nick resembled a version of the Pied Piper of Hamelin when he led the field trips. His enthusiasm when he talked about works of art made one realise that he instinctively looked at every painting or sculpture afresh each time he spoke, and new ideas would tumble from his lips.

When my two terms as chair came to an end six years later, I was reluctant to retire. I had loved every minute of it. A former chief curator, Gabriele Finaldi, had returned from the Prado and taken over as director. He was a popular figure with quite a different style to Nicholas Penny's. Behind his radiant smile and

Beaumont Group dinner in the Sala Grande, Palazzo Colonna, Rome, 2015

Nicholas Penny lecturing during a Beaumont Group study trip to Berlin, May 2011

relaxed manner was a shrewd determination to carry the Gallery forward to even more ambitious heights, including expanding the gallery spaces. Gabriele chose St Petersburg as the spring trip in 2019, as he knew Dr Piotrovsky, the director of the Hermitage. We found ourselves enjoying champagne and Russian Easter cake with Piotrovsky at the Hermitage on Easter Sunday morning. The new layout of the Winter Palace was his enlightened redistribution of the vast collections it encompasses. I was very pleased to be invited on a private visit to the print room with Katrin Henkel, who had been there on an earlier Beaumont trip and was able to get us in on that basis. Although in a decidedly shabby eighteenth-century stuccoed room reached up a simple back staircase, this was a major collection of drawings, and we did not have nearly long enough to do justice to it.

I had managed to round up three other people in the Circle who, like me, were keen to spend an extra day going to Novgorod, the medieval capital that had reached its peak in the fourteenth century and was famous for its many monasteries and churches. We had hired a minibus and a guide, but no one had thought to point out that because it was May Day, all of Russia would be not only on holiday but also on the roads. The ten-hour journey was made in bumper-to-bumper traffic, and I was not popular with my fellow-travellers when we finally got back to St Petersburg well after dark. I, at least, had enjoyed the icon museum and the few churches that were open, and the carefully restored red brick fortress. On the so-called 'motorway', we drove through abandoned villages whose old, unpainted wooden houses had simply collapsed on their haunches.

It was Gabriele's idea to introduce the Beaumont Circle to the riches of the Persian Gulf and, most particularly, to the Louvre of the East in Abu Dhabi in October 2019. With much sadness, John and I both missed this adventure due to illness – almost the only part of the Middle East we had not explored on our own.

The two annual events which draw the Beaumonts closest together are the Director's Dinner in the late autumn and the Open House in the spring. The Dinner is a gala in black tie, although the ladies' dresses have grown shorter with the passage of time. It is such a privilege to dine in a grand gallery hung with magnificent paintings of world renown, at tables laden with beautiful flowers. The convivial atmosphere is enhanced by the formal announcement of the destination for the May study trip, open to both groups. The choice of city alternates between northern and southern Europe. This is rarely as great a surprise as it is meant to be: somehow, word always gets out beforehand. The Open House is an evening for the director and the curators to thank the patrons yet again for their generous support of the Gallery. Each Beaumont may bring several guests to view a large selection of rooms, beautifully lit for the occasion, through which the curators give guided tours throughout the evening, in between drinks and canapés.

I very much enjoyed my turn as Chair. I had the necessary time to devote to it and loved the combined duties of attending all the events, which made it possible for me to indulge in my love of pictures, as well as acting as host to the patrons, through whom I made many interesting new friends. I also enjoyed working with the Development Department's charming staff, who were keen to ensure that I knew that X always wore a hat at the dinner whilst Y could never sit next to Z.

My experience as an art historian and as an art dealer had equipped me well for chairing the Beaumont Group. I had always loved meeting a wide variety of people and gathering them together in a mutual enjoyment of art. Everything I had done in my life up to this point, everything I had been passionate about, came to fruition in this role, and I felt a deep sense of fulfilment.

CHAPTER 25

John

The weekend before our annual family trip to Tuscany in the summer of 2015, John and I stayed with Phillip Ward Green, our old friend from my Cairo days, and his partner Tony Roper, on Dartmoor. At dinner on Saturday evening, the four of us unwisely got involved in a very heated argument over Israel and Palestine. Tony, who had been a young sapper in the Second World War, suddenly leapt to his feet and bellowed that he knew best because he had been present in the area at the end of the war. In that instant, John's face turned purple, and his chair tipped backwards to the floor. Indignant rage had led to a serious brain haemorrhage. An ambulance was immediately summoned, but the paramedics had great difficulty lifting John into their vehicle, which was jammed between the bushes lining the steep and narrow drive. The nightmare continued in Plymouth's Derriford Hospital, the brain trauma hospital for the southwest of England, for five weeks, while I stayed in a nearby Travelodge with Emily or Jocelyn. John's recovery then continued for another six weeks in the rehabilitation clinic at the National Hospital for Neurology and Neurosurgery in Queen's Square, near the British Museum. As he grew stronger, we were able to take him out in a wheelchair to family gatherings at local restaurants as well as trips to the British Museum and the Curzon Bloomsbury. It became a new way of life. During his stay in Queen's Square, John found himself able to read again and began to tackle seriously long and heavy books: a new life of Bernard Berenson, a new history of the Silk Routes, and his cousin Thomas Grant's first book, *Jeremy Hutchinson's Case Histories*. We were all greatly heartened by his progress.

Back at home, John recovered more slowly, as there were so many more challenges. The stroke had affected his ability to balance himself, and he had had to learn to walk again. He had to build the confidence to tackle the several flights of stairs in our house. However, by the following summer (2016), we were able to think of travelling again and thus retrieving something of our former lifestyle. We tentatively started with a return to Cornwall for the annual family holiday. John had happy memories of his own childhood holidays in Cornwall, and we spent a whole afternoon trying to find his Uncle Guillaume's large neoclassical house at Penryn, as well as his grave in one of the Truro cemeteries. Sadly, we could not find either, but we explored Truro Cathedral, where Guillaume had been the organist for over forty years, and found a plaque in his honour.

In September, John and I braced ourselves for a seven-hour journey by Eurostar to Avignon, where we stayed in great comfort opposite the Popes' Palace. In the evenings, we enjoyed the floodlit palace from our bedroom windows. With a stick, John managed to tour this huge palace with its endless high steps, but it was more than enough sightseeing for one day: the old habit of diving into multiple churches in the late afternoon had become too much. On another outing, a driver took us to the village of St Remy-de-Provence, where we had lunch in the main square with fresh chestnuts pelting down onto our table in the high wind. We walked to the former monastery of St-Paul-de-Mausole where Van Gogh had been confined for a year at his own request. John loved the tranquillity of this spot. We also tried Aix-en-Provence, but the narrow streets were too hot and confusing for John. The day was saved by a drive round the spectacular Mont Sainte-Victoire, so perfectly captured by Cézanne in both colour and shape, and a visit to the small and soothing Cistercian monastery of Silvacane on the way home. Our final day was spent at Villeneuve-lès-Avignon, just across the Rhône and known as the 'City of the Cardinals'. John had chosen this peaceful location, and we sat in the sun enjoying the atmosphere. His lifelong spirit of romanticism was still there, but his brain now tired quickly.

The Sirens sang again the following spring and we returned to La Foce, the writer Iris Origo's estate in Tuscany's Val d'Orcia, for a week in July, the landscape as breathtaking as ever. Jay and Frank came up from Rome to spend a day with us in nearby Montepulciano: by now, two churches and a good lunch were a major excursion for John.

The following summer, we returned to Provence with the family, but for John it was exhausting and proved to be the last family holiday abroad. We stayed in the pretty town of Lourmarin in the Luberon, and on the first day, when John had the most energy, Jocelyn drove us to see the Cistercian Abbaye Notre-Dame de Sénanque. It was a memorable outing, and, as we drove home, the sun was casting its golden evening glow over magnificent countryside. The rest of the week was largely a success, but John was completely defeated by the Pont du Gard – its scale overwhelmed him.

John and I travelled to Glasgow later that autumn, and from there to the Isle of Bute to see Mount Stuart House, seat of the Earls of Bute, and what remained of the famous Bute collection. Somehow John managed the train from Glasgow, then the boat, then the bus to the gates of Mount Stuart House, then a minibus to the door, and later that day, the whole journey in reverse, with the boat train waiting specially for us.

John had always been proud of his great-uncle John Singer Sargent, and towards the end of his life going to Sargent exhibitions became an even greater passion. When his brother Richard, a leading authority on Sargent, and the director of the Dulwich Gallery, Xavier Bray, organised a show of Sargent's watercolours in 2017 from English private collections, two generations of the extended Sargent family were invited to the opening and dinner afterwards. John put his best foot forward for this long evening. He was also adamant that all his young grandchildren should see this exhibition and understand their Sargent legacy. They came up from the depths of the country and were rewarded with paintboxes replicating Sargent's watercolours.

John had always got on well with my father's family and became increasingly fond of Eric Lubbock, who became 4th Lord Avebury in 1971 and was the son of Maurice, Granny Grant Duff's youngest brother. Eric was one of the cousins who had accompanied us on the boat to Canada in 1940. Having returned to England immediately after the war, he had followed in the footsteps of his grandfather John Lubbock, 1st Lord Avebury, by pursuing a Liberal Party career, and won from the Conservatives the famous Orpington by-election in 1962. However, most of his long parliamentary career was spent in the House of Lords and campaigning for human rights. I had remembered him in Canada as being much older (he was six years older) and very shy. My mother always said that our father, his first cousin, looked like him; this made him even more special to me. Eric had amazing blue eyes, which shone with pleasure when we turned up at his 86th birthday party only days after John's final release from hospital following his stroke. Just over a year later, we were among the few invited to attend Eric's Buddhist burial in the Lubbock family cemetery in the woods at High Elms. I was also able to get John to the Royal Institution and up the curving steps of the lecture theatre for Eric's commemoration a few months later. John was particularly delighted because his favourite Labour leader, Jeremy Corbyn, gave a eulogy.

Annina Lubbock, daughter of my Roman cousin Jocelyn Lubbock and great-niece of the writer Percy Lubbock, came back into our lives at this juncture and introduced us to the Pyms. John Pym, son of Victoria Lubbock, another cousin of Granny Grant Duff's, was brought up in Kent at Emmetts, the country house used for the film of E.M. Forster's *Room with a View*. The Lubbocks were very proud of this connection, in view of their deep attachment to Italy and their family ties with it. John Pym had spent memorable childhood holidays at Lerici visiting his uncle Percy. He encouraged Annina to compile an anthology of the experiences and anecdotes of the readers who had worked with Percy – who included the writer Quentin Crewe, and the art historians Hugh Honour and John Fleming. They were all very fond of this eminent literary figure who had, sadly, gone blind towards the end of his life. Some of the readers had written a more literary account of their experiences of reading to Percy, but John's mind was no longer clear enough for such an approach. Therefore, I simply asked him to describe his time there and why he had loved it so much. Here is a summary of what he said:

My introduction to reading to Percy Lubbock came through my parents' friend, Libby King, daughter of my father's childhood friend Conradine Hobhouse [a Grant Duff cousin of mine], who lived near us in Wiltshire. I was at a very loose end, and this was a perfect solution. I set off for Italy in the late summer of 1962. I remember my night train journey from Paris but, much more vividly, a vision in red smiling up at me from the station platform at La Spezia. This was Georgette Lubbock [wife of Jocelyn Lubbock] who had driven over to meet me from Percy's magical villa, Gli Scafari, near Lerici. She and Jocelyn, Percy's nephew, were to become life-long supporting friends.

Percy was very warm and welcoming. He was gently spoken and very civilized, although he did not suffer fools gladly. He also did not like being read to by women! He had a reputation among women for not being a womanizer. However, this did not stop women, for example Lady Dick-Lauder, who talked constantly about 'BB' [the art historian Bernard Berenson], from coming to pay him a visit. These ladies would sit in the drawing-room and enjoy being guests.

I would start reading about eight o'clock in the morning and then at about one there was a break for lunch with Georgette, if she were there, and alone, when she was in Rome. The first winter was very cold and Percy had a fire in his study. However, the butler would buy cheap coal and pocket the change, so the fire would often smoke. After lunch there was time to roam. Cecil Pinsent's garden was designed to give the impression of complete informality with a mass of lovely free-growing flowers. Beyond it, I could pick my way up to the top of the promontory and then down to the town of Sarzana through an abundance of fig trees – the figs were never picked. In the late autumn, orange persimmons added magnificent colour to the scene. In warm weather, there was an intoxicating scent of sweet herbs growing in the so-called macchia (the wild vegetation). In the evening I would read to Percy again or share his pleasure in listening to music on the gramophone. Percy particularly liked romantic music – Wagner, Brahms and Richard Strauss. As a young man, Percy went frequently to the opera, particularly in Germany. He had learnt German in Dresden before the First World War.

I read a variety of books to Percy. He liked Robert Louis Stevenson as a travel writer, but during my time one of his favourite books was a contemporary novel called *The Constant Nymph* written by Margaret Kennedy in 1924. I tried Henry James, but Percy did not like the way I read James aloud – neither the early nor the late novels – my Boston accent was not good enough! Percy much enjoyed poetry; sometimes he would choose it and sometimes he asked me to choose. He was especially keen on Thomas Hardy's love poems. However, the two books I remember reading most often were Milton's *Paradise Lost* and Gibbon's *Decline and Fall of the Roman Empire*. I read them many times, as Percy would remark – after a few days of my trying something else, 'It is a long time since I have heard Milton or Gibbon'. Thus, to vary the flow, I would read the excellent footnotes to Gibbon's Decline and Fall and we would discuss them in detail. They became almost the best part of the book!

Percy was also interested in all aspects of Christianity. I would be asked to read early nineteenth-century commentaries on the Bible, which Percy knew well. We were both very interested in the Oxford Movement and Percy particularly enjoyed Loss and Gain, the first novel by Cardinal Newman in which he describes his own path to faith. However, our discussions were limited because Percy was not the sort of person you could disagree with except as a joke. For example, he firmly objected to the idea of papal infallibility.

Sometimes we would talk at random. Percy would have met E.M. Forster while reading English Literature at Kings College, Cambridge. He always referred to Forster as Morgan. One day Percy dictated a letter to me inviting Morgan to stay at Lerici. In the letter, Percy treated him rather like a joke and pointed out that he, Forster, had achieved a scholarly thesis being written on his books whereas Percy never had! In his reply, Forster pointed out that several theses had been written on his books, and addressed Percy rather distantly as Perceval. I received the impression that Percy was hurt by this response, especially as Forster did not acknowledge the invitation to stay.

Percy had an interesting rapport with certain women. He had written about his marriage to Iris Origo's mother, Lady Sybil Scott, and he talked to me about their relationship. Percy was, of course, very fond of Edith Wharton and talked to me about her and how they had travelled together – especially in North Africa. In contrast, I felt that in his relationship with Henry James, Percy treated him more as a god.

Although Percy was sadly almost blind, he could distinguish colours, as I discovered to my cost. Often very witty, he caught me out one very hot summer's afternoon. I naughtily turned up in a bathing-suit as I thought Percy would not know. His first words were to ask if I was wearing a 'pink shirt'!

The last two years of John's life were spent quietly at home in Cheyne Row, the house we moved to in 2012, near the church where we had been married. The idea of being so near to where his father had been brought up and where he used to visit his grandmother from school gave him great pleasure. He loved walking to Tite Street to see Sargent's house and studio and then on to the Physic Garden for a picnic lunch. The garden was his choice for his 80th birthday party, and continued to give him joy. He was able to walk there until the end of August 2020. His growing dementia was a serious affliction, but I was convinced that he and I never lost touch – to the point where I felt guilty every time I went out on my own. Some observers might have thought he was not actually comprehending a conversation, but he usually was! From 2018 I had taken on three South African carers: Nolitha first, who then invited her friend Anathi to share the days, and later Nolitha's husband Ronald (actually from Zimbabwe), who took on the nights. They loved John and were the only three people we saw all through the first Covid-19 lockdown. The days were long in every sense, so they would prepare late-night dinners to be enjoyed in the garden, set up programmes of opera and ballet on television whenever possible, and Ronald and John would sit and read the papers together in the drawing room. Best were the days when we could make John laugh, and Anathi always won the prize for the greatest success!

Epilogue

Very sadly, John died of Covid-19 in January 2021, contracted in a nearby care home where we had had to place him in December 2020 when he became unable to walk. We had been married for nearly fifty-three years and were always great companions. I was very gregarious, whilst he was relatively shy, but we complemented each other. He would listen intently to all conversation and was quick to supply forgotten facts from his extraordinary memory, as well as to quietly add unexpected insights and observations on all sorts of subjects. He was a very kind person and adored his children. John's love of music was reflected in the music Emily and Jocelyn chose for his funeral, which included Bach's *Prelude and Fugue in E Minor*, also played at the funeral of John's beloved Uncle Guillaume. As I sat in the church,

Jocelyn and Emily in the Protestant Cemetery, Rome, October 2021

listening, I became strangely aware of our wedding held so many years before in the same church, Our Most Holy Redeemer and St Thomas More. On that occasion, the beautiful music had been chosen by John, and I had been part of the spectacle. Now, at John's funeral service, I suddenly realised that I was the spectator and that I was actually occupying the seat where John's mother had sat on our wedding day, blowing kisses. It was uncanny, and the occasion the very opposite of that happy one fifty-three years before. We had come full circle: never could we have imagined finishing our long and varied life together in a house so near to the church where it had begun.

At the end of October 2021, Emily and Jocelyn and I made a pilgrimage to Lerici – and stayed under the eaves at Gli Scafari, where John had read to Percy Lubbock. The villa has now been turned into flats. We found it breathtakingly beautiful even in its modernised state. We had taken John's ashes with us to pour into the 'wine-dark' sea as if from a Grecian urn. We chose the rocks from which John and all the Villa's guests used to swim and we watched the waves carry the ashes away. At last we knew he was at peace. We went on to Rome for a celebration of his life in front of the plaque which had been inscribed for him and placed on one of the ancient walls in the Protestant Cemetery near the grave of Keats and the urn holding Shelley's heart. Also buried nearby are Jocelyn Lubbock and Laurie Pasqualino, Barbara and Fortunato's eldest daughter, and an old friend from our Rome days, John Opie, who had died only a few months earlier. Thus, surrounded by cypress trees and the graves of old friends in his beloved Rome, John will be remembered forever.

Index

Page numbers in *italics* refer to illustrations.

This edition first published in the UK by Unicorn
an imprint of Unicorn Publishing Group, 2022
Charleston Studio
Meadow Business Centre
Lewes BN8 5RW

www.unicornpublishing.org

10 9 8 7 6 5 4 3 2 1

ISBN 978-1-914414-94-7

Cover design by Unicorn Publishing Group
Typeset by Vivian Head
Printed in Malta by Gutenberg Press Ltd